**SESSION 1**

The Revelation of the Father

The Home Run Derby: Mantle vs. Mays

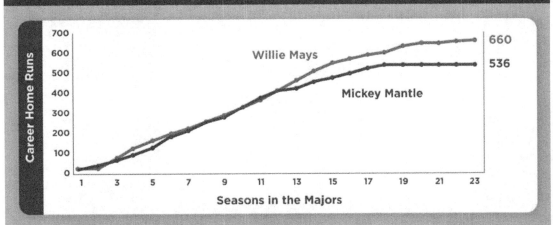

> It would have been hard to look him in the eye and say, 'Dad, I'm an alcoholic.' I don't think I could have done it. I would feel like I'd let him down. I don't know how you get over that; I can't hit a home run for him anymore.
>
> Mickey Mantle

> [My sons] all drank too much because of me. We don't have normal father-son relationships. When they were growing up, I was playing baseball, and after I retired I was too busy traveling around being Mickey Mantle. We never played catch in the backyard. But when they were old enough to drink, we became drinking buddies.
>
> Mickey Mantle

The Four Leadership Roles of Men

Political Leadership	Harmoniously order society to peace.	Men's Leadership Roles	Live in union with God to receive His blessings.	Moral Leadership
Economic Leadership	Make the earth fruitful, which is tied to the fruitfulness of the womb.		Battle Satan over the family, the channel of grace.	Military Leadership

A Sustainable Socioeconomic Model

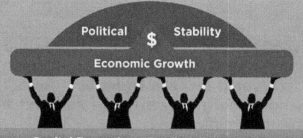

Political $ Stability

Economic Growth

Human Capital Formation - Family & Formal Education

God

The 7 Steps of That Man Is You!

TMIY — THAT MAN IS YOU!

1. Honor your wedding vows
2. Use money for others
3. Give God some of your time
4. Set your mind on things above
5. Find God in yourself
6. Find God in other people
7. Practice Superabundant Mercy

TMIY

TMIY — THAT MAN IS YOU!

SESSION 1

- **What father-son story do you know that is similar to the Mickey Mantle story?**

- **How can you be the father your children truly need you to be?**

- *Who are you going to bring with you next week?*

Next Week
The Heart of a Father

SESSION 2

The Happiness of Children

The Desire to be Happy

There is no man who does not desire [happiness], and each one desires it with such earnestness that he prefers it to all other things; whoever, in fact, desires other things, desires them for this end alone.

St. Augustine
Sermon 306, 3

TMIY

The Wanderings of St. Augustine

So for the space of nine years (from my nineteenth to my twenty-eighth year) I lived a life in which I was seduced and seducing, deceived and deceiving, the prey of various desires. My public life was that of a teacher of what are called the 'liberal arts.' In private I went under cover of a false kind of religion. I was arrogant in the one sphere, superstitious in the other, and vain and empty from all points of view.

St. Augustine
Confessions, Book IV, Chapter 1

TMIY

The Conversion of St. Augustine

A huge storm rose up within me... Suddenly, a voice reaches my ears from a nearby house... 'Take it and read it'... I snatched up the book, opened it, and read in silence the passage upon which my eyes first fell: 'Not in rioting and drunkenness, not in chambering and wantonness, not is strife and envying; but put ye on the Lord Jesus Christ, and make not provision for the flesh in concupiscence.' I had no wish to read further; there was no need to.

Confessions, Book VIII, Chapter 12

TMIY

The Happiness of St. Augustine

Late have I loved thee, beauty ever ancient, ever new, late have I loved thee! You were within me and I was outside, and there I sought for you and in my ugliness I plunged into the beauties that you have made. You were with me, and I was not with you... You called, you cried out, you shattered my deafness: you flashed, you shone, you scattered my blindness: you breathed perfume, and I drew in my breath and I pant for you: I tasted, and I am hungry and thirsty... When in my whole self I shall cling to you united, I shall find no sorrow anywhere, no labor; wholly alive will my life be all full of you.

St. Augustine
Confessions, Book X, Chapters 27-28

TMIY

College Degree

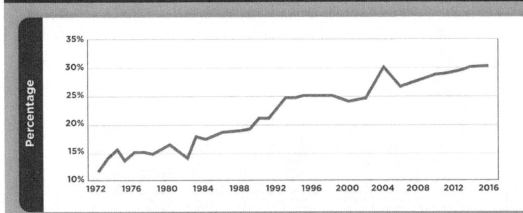

Source: General Social Survey, 1972-2016.

TMIY

No Religious Affiliation (Aged 18-24)

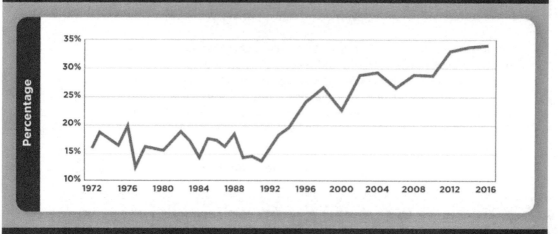

Source: General Social Survey, 1972-2016.

TMIY

Married (Aged 18-24)

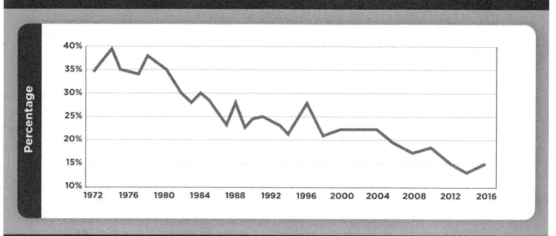

Source: General Social Survey, 1972-2016.

TMIY

Time to Initiate Sex with Current Partner

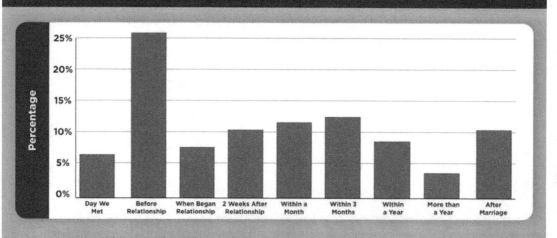

Source: Regnerus, M., "Cheap Sex: The Transformation of Men, Marriage, and Monogamy," Oxford University Press, 2017, Figure 3.2, p. 97.

TMIY

Happiness (Aged 18-24)

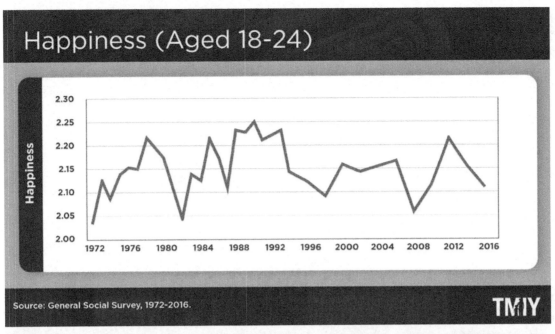

Source: General Social Survey, 1972-2016.

The Determinants of Happiness

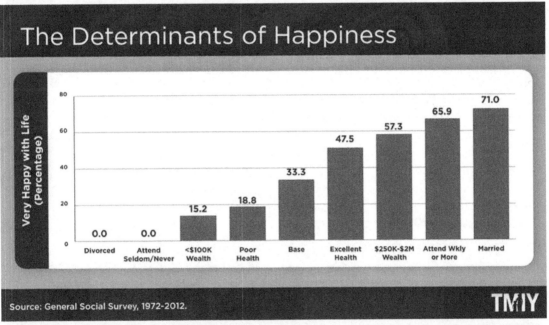

Source: General Social Survey, 1972-2012.

The Simple Answer for Happiness

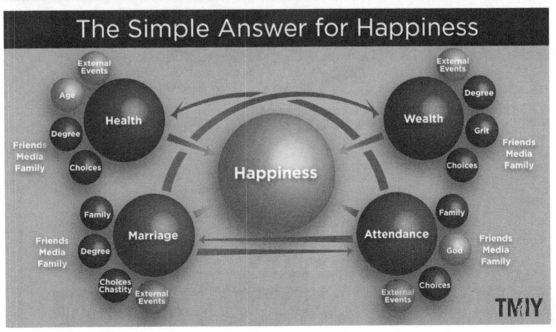

Excellent Health

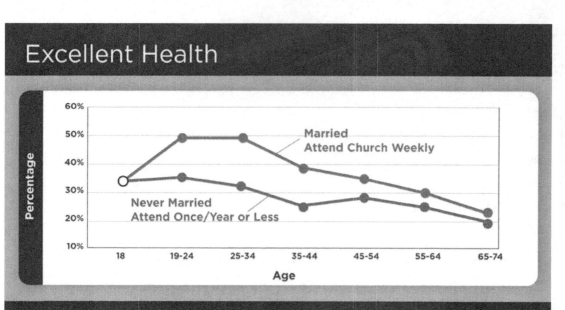

Married
Attend Church Weekly

Never Married
Attend Once/Year or Less

Source: General Social Survey, 1972-2016.

TMIY

Wealth

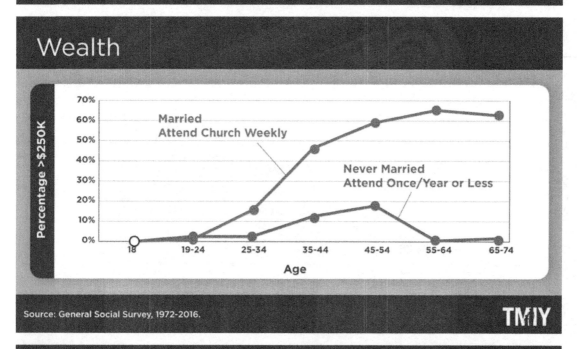

Married
Attend Church Weekly

Never Married
Attend Once/Year or Less

Source: General Social Survey, 1972-2016.

TMIY

Very Happy in Life

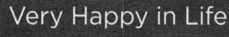

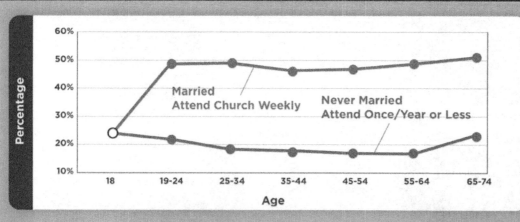

Married
Attend Church Weekly

Never Married
Attend Once/Year or Less

Source: General Social Survey, 1972-2016.

TMIY

SESSION 2

- How do you define happiness? How happy are you?

- How can you better place faith and family as the foundation of your life and your children's lives?

Next Week

That Man is You!
Taking the Next Step

SESSION 3

To Be a Father

The Neurochemistry of a Thought

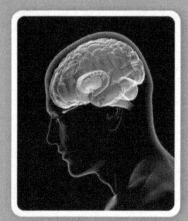

- Electrochemical travels down membrane of neuron.
- Calcium concentration increases in presynaptic membrane.
- Vesicles release neurotransmitter into synapse.
- Neurotransmitter binds to receptor cells in the postsynaptic cells.
- Receptor molecules are activated.
- Receptor cells are cleared of neurotransmitter.
- Neurotransmitter is reabsorbed or broken down.
- Understanding the mind-brain interaction: "the greatest adventure of my life."
- Are neurotransmitters thoughts? Is the transfer of a bit of information consciousness?

TMIY

A Spiritual-Physical Reality

> The essential feature... is that the mind and brain are independent entities... and that they interact by quantum physics... There is a frontier, and across this frontier there is interaction in both directions, which can be conceived as a flow of information, not of energy. Thus we have the extraordinary doctrine that the world of matter-energy is not completely sealed.

Source: Eccles, J., "How the Self Controls Its Brain," Springer-Verlag, 1994, p. 9.

TMIY

The Mystery of the Human Person

"The human person, created in the image of God, is a being at once corporeal and spiritual. The biblical account expresses this reality in symbolic language when it affirms that 'then the LORD God formed man of dust from the ground, and breathed into his nostrils the breath of life'" (Catechism #362).

"Man 'is capable of self-knowledge, of self-possession and of freely giving himself and entering into communion with other persons" (Catechism #357).

TMIY

The Four Types of Formation

Human Formation

Natural formation of the material nature of man.

Intellectual Formation

Formation of the human intellect to embrace truth.

Pastoral Formation

Formation in mercy to live together harmoniously.

Moral Formation

Spiritual formation of the will to embrace the good.

Body · Intellect (Consciousness) · Human Person · Relationships · Will (Freedom)

TMIY

The Determinants of Happiness

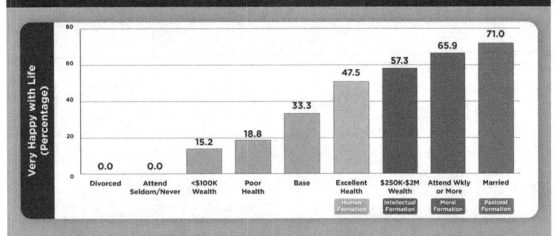

Source: General Social Survey, 1972-2012.

TMIY

3-2

A Code of Conduct

> The will to prepare is the juncture of where it all happens. It is about the player who can get out of bed at 6:15 in the morning when he is sore and he is stiff and he does not want to practice. But he goes to practice. And he gears up and does his best totally in every drill of that practice. The will to prepare is what develops the discipline and the know-how that transforms itself on game day into the will to win.
>
> **Bud Wilkinson**

TMIY

A Code of Conduct on a Higher Level

> The most amazing development prevented rather than instituted an upset; TCU attempted a pass into the OU end zone and was credited with a touchdown, but TCU Captain Johnny Crouch honestly confessed that the ball had bounced before it was gathered in. Thus, in the end, enabling OU to win.
>
> *Sports Illustrated*
> **October 4, 1954**

TMIY

THAT MAN IS YOU

SESSION 3

- When was the most difficult time that you had to do the right thing? What happened?

- When has one of your children done the right thing when it was most difficult? What did you do?

Next Week

The Heart of a Father

The Heart of a Father

St. Therese: Doctor of the Church

The core of her message is actually the mystery itself of God-Love, of the Triune God... At the summit, as the source and goal, is the merciful love of the three Divine Persons... At the root, on the subject's part, is the experience of being the Father's adoptive children in Jesus; this is the most authentic meaning of spiritual childhood, that is, the experience of divine filiation, under the movement of the Holy Spirit.

Pope St. John Paul II
Divini Amoris Scientia, #8
October 19, 1997

TMIY

An Image of the Merciful Father

"I looked more frequently at Papa than at the preacher, for his handsome face said so much to me! His eyes, at times, were filled with tears which he tried in vain to stop; he seemed no longer held by earth, so much did his soul love to lose itself in the eternal truths."

"What shall I say of the winter evenings at home, especially the Sunday evenings? Ah! how I loved... to sit with Celine on Papa's knees. He used to sing, in his beautiful voice, airs that filled the soul with profound thoughts, or else, rocking us gently, he recited poems that taught the eternal truths. Then we all went upstairs to say our night prayers together and the little Queen was alone near her King, having only to look at him to see how the saints pray."

Source: "Story of a Soul – The Autobiography of St. Therese of Lisieux," 3rd Edition, Translated by Clarke, J., ICS Publications, 1996, p. 42 and p. 43.

The Little Way of St. Therese

"I know, O Mother full of grace, that you lived in great poverty in Nazareth. You did not long to leave it; no raptures, miracles or ecstasies lightened your life... you chose to tread the everyday paths so as to show little ones the way to heaven."

"I applied myself to practicing little virtues, not having the capability of practicing the great."

"At home, our education had piety as its chief lever. There was a complete liturgy of household life."

Source: Quoted in Longenecker, D., "St. Benedict and St. Therese – The Little Rule and the Little Way," Our Sunday Visitor Publishing Division, 2002, p. 175.
"Story of a Soul – The Autobiography of St. Therese of Lisieux," 3rd Edition, Translated by Clarke, J., ICS Publications, 1996, p. 159.
Martin, C., "The Father of the Little Flower," Tan Books and Publishers, Inc., Rockford, IL, 2005, p. 47.

TMIY

The Holiness of St. Therese

"Jesus knew I was too feeble to be exposed to temptation... I have no merit at all, then, in not having given myself up to the love of creatures. I was preserved from it only through God's mercy! I know that without Him, I could have fallen as low as St. Mary Magdalene, and the profound words of Our Lord to Simon resound with a great sweetness in my soul. I know that 'he to whom less is forgiven loves less,' but I also know that Jesus has forgiven me more than St. Mary Magdalene since He forgave me in advance by preventing me from falling."

"I remember that when he used to take me to the Benedictine School, my teachers, the nuns, used to say he reminded them of St. Joseph. Indeed he was truly a just man, and when I wish to picture what St. Joseph was like, I just like to think of my father."

Source: "Story of a Soul – The Autobiography of St. Therese of Lisieux," 3rd Edition, Translated by Clarke, J., ICS Publications, 1996, p. 83.
Martin, C., "The Father of the Little Flower," Tan Books and Publishers, Inc., Rockford, IL, 2005, p. 55.

TMIY

The Sacrifice of St. Therese

"In order to live in one single act of perfect Love, I OFFER MYSELF AS A VICTIM OF HOLOCAUST TO YOUR MERCIFUL LOVE, asking You to consume me incessantly, allowing the waves of infinite tenderness shut up within You to overflow into my soul, and that thus I may become a martyr of Your Love, O my God!"

"I do not regret having surrendered myself to Love. Oh no! I don't regret it; just the opposite!"

"I am too happy, it isn't possible to go to heaven this way. I want to suffer something for you! I offer myself... the word victim died on his lips."

Source: "Story of a Soul – The Autobiography of St. Therese of Lisieux," 3rd Edition, Translated by Clarke, J., ICS Publications, 1996, p. 177, p. 170, p. 154 footnote.

TMIY

Discovering the Father's Love

> "I understood that the Church had a Heart and that this Heart was burning with love. I understood it was Love alone that made the Church's members act, that if Love ever became extinct, apostles would not preach the Gospel and martyrs would no shed their blood. I understood that Love comprised all vocations, that love was everything, that it embraced all times and places... im a word, t hat it was eternal. Then in the excess of my delirious joy, I cried out: O Jesus, my Love... My vocation, at last I have found it... My vocation is love."

> "I cannot say how much I loved Papa; everything in him caused me to admire him. When he explained his ideas to me... I told him very simply that surely if he said this to the great men of the government, they would take him to make him King... but in the bottom of my heart I was happy that it was only myself who knew Papa well, for if he became King of France... he would no longer be my King alone."

Source: "Story of a Soul – The Autobiography of St. Therese of Lisieux," 3rd Edition, Translated by Clarke, J., ICS Publications, 1996, p. 194 and p. 46.

TMIY

The Transformation of the Person

Transforming the Body

- Body and soul are integrated.
- Body participates in spiritual reality of person.
  - Unhealthy relationships lead to stress.
  - Stress leads to illness in the body.
- Epigenetics: Behavior changes gene expression.
  - Alcoholism has an epigenetic expression.
  - Children of alcoholics are more likely to be alcoholic.

Consciousness and Memory

- The brain is transformed by experience.
- Feedback loop in reward system either reinforces or avoids behavior for the future.
- The brain anticipates rewards based on past behavior and builds a tolerance for repeated behaviors.
- The building of "virtue" or "vice".

Wiring Brains

- Relationships are hardwired as an ultimate good.
- Immature brain uses other brains to organize its own thought processes.
- Mirror neuron system brings other people's actions into our own brain.
- Love links two brains to share goods.
- Emotional pain is physical pain.

The Reward System

- The Will seeks to act and is guided by the brain's reward system.
- Caudate Nucleus drives brain to the "good."
- "Goods" are hardwired and/or learned through experience.
- The brain is rewarded with dopamine when it achieves its good.

Body · Intellect (Consciousness) · Human Person · Will (Freedom) · Relationships

TMIY

Nature and Nurture

> " The consensus, then, is that genes account for about half of one's IQ... this leaves the other half to the environment... With much of the evidence that early experience is critical to a child's later intellectual potential. "

Source: Eliot, E., "What's Going on in There? How the Brain and Mind Develop in the First Five Years of Life," Bantam Books, New York, 1999, p. 425-427.

TMIY

The Formation of the Child

 The body of the child flows out from "who we are."

"Except for a few cognitive instincts, newborns pretty much just perceive and react... Cognitive development is the product of two interacting influences – brain growth and experience."

"The brain continues to change in response to experience throughout the lifespan. We are in lifelong development, as reflected in the every-changing structure of the brain throughout our lives... attachment relationships are the major environmental factors that shape brain development during its period of maximal growth."

Experience – especially of interpersonal relationships.

The Mirror Neuron System

Source: Eliot, E., "What's Going on in There? How the Brain and Mind Develop in the First Five Years of Life," Bantam Books, New York, 1999, p. 392.
Siegel, D., "The Developing Mind: How Relationships and the Brain interact to Shape Who We Are," 2nd Edition, The Guilford Press, New York, 2012, pp. 35 and 112.

TMIY

An Issue of the Heart

 The serpent was more subtle than any other wild creature that the LORD God had made. He said to the woman, "Did God say, `You shall not eat of any tree of the garden`?... You will not die. For God knows that when you eat of it your eyes will be opened, and you will be like God, knowing good and evil." So when the woman saw that the tree was good for food, and that it was a delight to the eyes, and that the tree was to be desired to make one wise, she took of its fruit and ate; and she also gave some to her husband, and he ate.

Genesis 3:1-6

TMIY

A Changed Reality

 "And the eyes of them both were opened: and when they perceived themselves to be naked, they sewed together fig leaves, and made themselves clothes. And when they heard the voice of the Lord God walking in paradise at the afternoon air, Adam and his wife hid themselves from the face of the Lord God amidst the trees of paradise" (Genesis 3:7-8).

 "Your desire shall be for your husband, and he shall rule over you" (Genesis 3:16).

 "Because you... have eaten of the tree of which I commanded you, 'You shall not eat of it,' cursed is the ground because of you... In the sweat of your face you shall eat bread till you return to the ground, for out of it your were taken; you are dust and to dust you shall return" (Genesis 3:17-19).

TMIY

The Story of Cain and Abel

> In the course of time Cain brought to the LORD an offering of the fruit of the ground, and Abel brought of the firstlings of his flock and of their fat portions. And the LORD had regard for Abel and his offering, but for Cain and his offering he had no regard... Cain said to Abel is brother, "Let us go out to the field." And when they were in the field, Cain rose up against his brother Abel, and killed him.
>
> **Genesis 4:3-8**

TMIY

Cain as a Reflection of Adam's Heart

Adam	Cain
1 "The LORD God took the man and put him in the garden of Eden to till it" (Genesis 2:15).	**1** "Cain [was] a tiller of the ground" (Genesis 4:2).
2 "Cursed is the ground because of you ... thorns and thistles it shall bring forth to you" (Genesis 3:17-18).	**2** "You are cursed from the ground... When you till the ground, it shall no longer yield to you its strength" (Genesis 4:11-12).
3 "[Adam] and [Eve] hid themselves from the presence of the LORD God" (Genesis 3:8).	**3** "From thy face I shall be hidden" (Genesis 4:14).
4 "God sent him forth from the garden of Eden" (Genesis 3:23).	**4** "You shall be a fugitive and a wanderer on the earth" (Genesis 4:12).

TMIY

THAT MAN IS YOU!   **SESSION 4**

- Consider Louis Martin and his impact on Therese. What is the one thing you would like your children to get from you? What actions do you need to take to make that a reality?

- Consider Cain. What actions do you need to stop before they're handed on to your children?

Next Week

Don Bosco: The Apostle to Youth

SESSION 5

Don Bosco:
The Apostle to Youth

The Dream of St. John Bosco

> Don Bosco dreamed that he was "in a field surrounded by a crowd of boys. Some... were fighting and using bad language. On hearing the language he lost his temper, dashed in among them and laid about him with his fists... and a battle royal began... In the middle of this ruckus appeared a noble-looking Man... 'Come here,' he said... 'You will never help these boys by beating them. Be kind to them, lead them, teach them that sin is evil and that purity is a precious gift.'... 'Who are you to tell me to do all these difficult things?' Don Bosco demanded. 'I am the Son of the woman your mother taught you to salute three times a day... By listening to the woman I shall send to you, you will do everything with ease.' The Man disappeared and the boys at once changed into dogs, wolves and other wild animals. Trembling with fear, he turned to find a beautiful and gracious Lady at his side. 'Don't be afraid,' she said... 'What I shall do for these animals, you must do for all my children'... When she had finished speaking, he saw that the wild animals had indeed been changed to lambs... Confused by what he saw, he started to cry, 'I don't understand!' 'Do not worry, my child,' the Lady comforted him. 'You will understand everything in good time.'"

Source: Eccles, J., "How the Self Controls Its Brain," Springer-VerlSource: Lappin, P., "Give Me Souls: Life of Don Bosco," Salesiana Publishers, New York, 1986, "The Lady and the Dream, prior to Chapter 1. ag, 1994, p. 9.

A Parenting System For the Home

> This system is based entirely on reason and religion, and above all on kindness; therefore it excludes all violent punishment, and tries to do without even the slightest chastisement... The practice of this system is based entirely on these words of St. Paul: 'Love is patient, is kind... bears with all things, hopes all things, endures all things... Hence only a Christian can apply the 'Preventive System' with success.
>
> **Don Bosco**

Source: Lemoyne, G., "The Biographical Memoirs of St. John Bosco," v. 4, Salesiana Publishers, Inc., New York, 1967, pp. 381-382.

A Christian Parenting System

The preventative system consists in making the laws known and then watching carefully so that the pupils may at all times be under the vigilant eye of the Rector, who like loving fathers can... place the pupils in the impossibility of committing faults.

Don Bosco

Source: Lemoyne, G., "The Biographical Memoirs of St. John Bosco," v. 4, Salesiana Publishers, Inc., New York, 1967, p. 381.

TMIY

A Joyful Parenting System

Let the boys have full liberty to jump, run, and shout as much as they please... 'Do whatever you like,' the great friend of youth, St. Philip Neri, used to say, 'provided that you do not sin.'

Don Bosco

Source: Lemoyne, G., "The Biographical Memoirs of St. John Bosco," v. 4, Salesiana Publishers, Inc., New York, 1967, pp. 382-383.

TMIY

Holy Family   Seven Steps

	Holy Family		Seven Steps
The Niddah Laws (Cf. Leviticus 15:19)	1	1	Honor your wedding vows
Separation of the Challah (Cf. Numbers 15:20)	2	2	Use money for others
The Nerot Laws (Exodus 20:8)	3	3	Give God some of your time
The angel is sent to open Mary and Joseph's mind to God's presence in the home	4	4	Set your mind on things above
Mary is told she will find God in herself	5	5	Find God in yourself
Joseph is told he will find God in another person	6	6	Find God in other people
The Christian home is born when Joseph chooses the pathway to mercy and receives Mary into his home	7	7	Practice Superabundant Mercy

TMIY

Developing the Spirit of Nazareth

Abiding Presence	"Jesus went down with them and came to Nazareth, and was obedient to them" (Luke 2:51).
Joyful Service	"Whoever would be great among you must be your servant... even as the Son of man came not to be served but to serve" (Matthew 20:26-28).
Loving Sacrifice	"Jesus loved them to the end." "I lay down my life... No one takes it from me, but I lay it down of my own accord" (John 13:1 and John 10:17-18).

TMIY

The 7 Steps of That Man Is You!

TMIY
THAT MAN IS YOU!

1. Honor your wedding vows
2. Use money for others
3. Give God some of your time
4. Set your mind on things above
5. Find God in yourself
6. Find God in other people
7. Practice Superabundant Mercy

TMIY

Special Challenges for Youth

"The greatest vigilance shall be exercised to prevent dangerous companions, bad books, or persons who indulge in bad conversation from entering the institute. A good doorkeeper is a treasure for a house of education."

"I looked up and read these words: 'The place of no reprieve.' I realized that we were at the gates of hell... At intervals, many other lads came tumbling down [to hell] after them. I saw one unlucky boy being pushed down the slope by an evil companion. Others fell singly or with others, arm in arm or side by side. Each of them bore the name of his sin on his forehead... Again the portals would open thunderously and slam shut with a rumble. Then, dead silence! 'Bad companions, bad books and bad habits,' my guide exclaimed, 'are mainly responsible for so many eternally lost.'"

Source: Lemoyne, G., "The Biographical Memoirs of St. John Bosco," v. 4, Salesiana Publishers, Inc., New York, 1967, pp. 381-382. Brown, E., "Dreams, Visions and Prophecies of Don Bosco," Don Bosco Publications, New York, 1986, pp. 216-217.

TMIY

The Simple Answer for Happiness

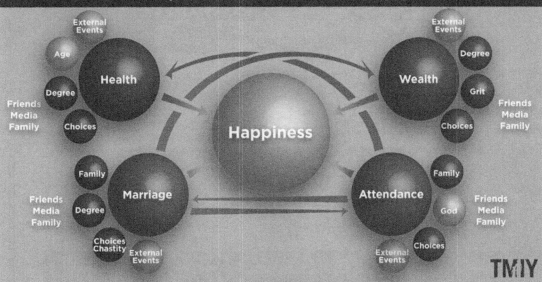

The Challenge of Formation

Human Formation
- Relates to laws of nature and the needs of the material human body.
- Body participates in spiritual reality of person.
- Epigenetics: Behavior changes gene expression.
- Friends and the media have a large influence on behaviors that impact the material body.
- The need for virtue.

Intellectual Formation
- Relates to the brain's desire to know the truth.
- The brain is transformed by experience.
- Feedback loop in reward system either reinforces or avoids behavior for the future.
- The brain anticipates rewards based on past behavior and builds a tolerance for repeated behaviors – building "virtue" or "vice".

Pastoral Formation
- Relates to the communal dimension of the human person and hardwired as a true good.
- Brain uses other brains to organize its own thought processes.
- Mirror neuron system brings other people's actions into our own brain.
- Friends have a large influence.
- Media images condition desire for communion.

Moral Formation
- Relates to human freedom.
- Driven by the brain's reward system.
- Desire to obtain the "good" – determined by hardwiring and experience.
- Conditioned by relationship with God and other people – family and friends; images placed in the brain – especially by the media.

(Center diagram: Human Person — Body, Intellect (Consciousness), Will (Freedom), Relationships)

The Little Way... of Love

"I know, O Mother full of grace, that you lived in great poverty in Nazareth. You did not long to leave it; no raptures, miracles or ecstasies lightened your life... you chose to tread the everyday paths so as to show little ones the way to heaven."

"I applied myself to practicing little virtues, not having the capability of practicing the great."

Source: Quoted in Longenecker, D., "St. Benedict and St. Therese - The Little Rule and the Little Way," Our Sunday Visitor Publishing Division, 2002, p. 175.
"Story of a Soul - The Autobiography of St. Therese of Lisieux," 3rd Edition, Translated by Clarke, J., ICS Publications, 1996, p. 159.

TMIY

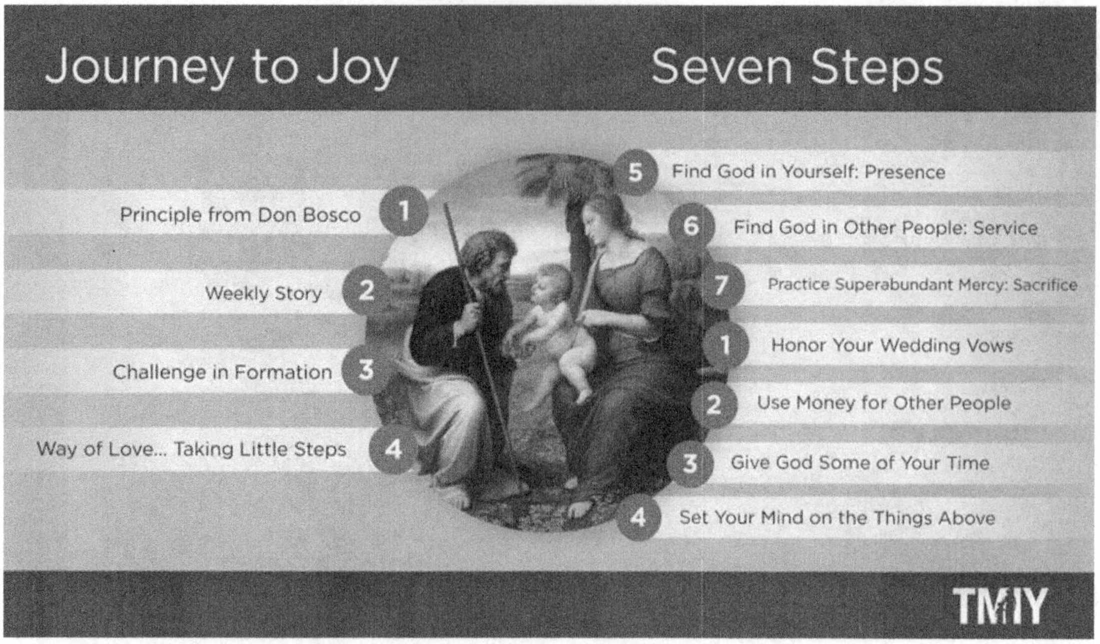

Journey to Joy   Seven Steps

Principle from Don Bosco **1**

Weekly Story **2**

Challenge in Formation **3**

Way of Love... Taking Little Steps **4**

5 Find God in Yourself: Presence

6 Find God in Other People: Service

7 Practice Superabundant Mercy: Sacrifice

1 Honor Your Wedding Vows

2 Use Money for Other People

3 Give God Some of Your Time

4 Set Your Mind on the Things Above

TMIY

TMIY
THAT MAN IS YOU!

SESSION 5

• How present are you to family? Physically present? Mentally and/or emotionally present?

• Is your home currently filled with joy? What brings your family the most joy? How can you bring more joy into your family?

Next Week

Week 1: Abiding Presence

TM1Y SESSION 6

Step 1: Abiding Presence

Journey to Joy   Seven Steps

Don Bosco: Abiding Presence **1**	**5** Find God in Yourself: Presence
	6 Find God in Other People: Service
Story: Grady Donaldson **2**	**7** Practice Superabundant Mercy: Sacrifice
	1 Honor Your Wedding Vows: Purity
Challenge: Time Crunch **3**	**2** Use Money for Other People: Virtue
	3 Give God Some of Your Time: Friends
Way of Joy: Be Present **4**	**4** Set Your Mind on Things Above: Wisdom

TM1Y

The Challenge of Formation

Human Formation

- Relates to laws of nature and the needs of the material human body.
- Body participates in spiritual reality of person.
- Epigenetics: Behavior changes gene expression.
- Friends and the media have a large influence on behaviors that impact the material body.
- The need for virtue.

Intellectual Formation

- Relates to the brain's desire to know the truth.
- The brain is transformed by experience.
- Feedback loop in reward system either reinforces or avoids behavior for the future.
- The brain anticipates rewards based on past behavior and builds a tolerance for repeated behaviors – building "virtue" or "vice".

Pastoral Formation

- Relates to the communal dimension of the human person and hardwired as a true good.
- Brain uses other brains to organize its own thought processes.
- Mirror neuron system brings other people's actions into our own brain.
- Friends have a large influence.
- Media images condition desire for communion.

Moral Formation

- Relates to human freedom.
- Driven by the brain's reward system.
- Desire to obtain the "good" – determined by hardwiring and experience.
- Conditioned by relationship with God and other people – family and friends; images placed in the brain – especially by the media.

Body — Intellect (Consciousness) — Human Person — Relationships — Will (Freedom)

TM1Y

Finding God in Yourself

- Grady Donaldson and twin brother Frank are born prematurely in 1922 (3 pounds each) in Adamsville, TN. Doctor told them, "Love them while you can because it won't be long."
- Somehow they survived.
- Grady had an engaging personality: everyone anticipated a career in politics – probably the governor or a senator. Some thought success in business.
- Went to WWII and served in Patton's 3rd Army.
- Both were captured in the Battle of the Bulge and sent to concentration camp in 1944.
- While in the concentration camp, Frank becomes very ill.
- Grady prays to God: "Let me and my brother go back to Adamsville alive, and I will never ask for anything again and accept whatever you give me."
- They both survived and returned to Adamsville. Grady accepted first job offered him – worker in a garment factory for minimum wage. Stayed the rest of his life.
- Wife worked in same garment factory and they had a wonderful marriage and life.
- Grady was loved and respected by everyone in town.
- His word was good as gold: "I respect your dad more than any man I've ever met, because... he kept his word forever."

Source: Russert, T., "Wisdom of Our Fathers," Random House Trade Paperbacks, New York, 2007, pp. 42-43.

TMIY

Our Promise to God

- "Have you come here to enter into Marriage without coercion, freely and wholeheartedly?"
- "Are you prepared, as you follow the path of Marriage, to love and honor each other for as long as you both shall live?"
- "Are you prepared to accept children lovingly from God and to bring them up according to the law of Christ and his Church?"

TMIY

The Influence of Parents on Children

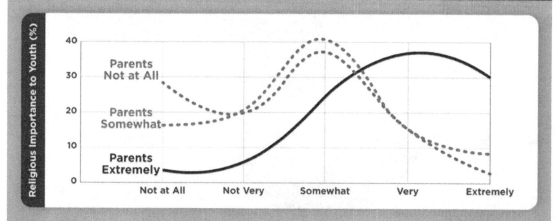

Source: Smith, C., et al., "Soul Searching: The Religious and Spiritual Lives of American Teenagers," Oxford University Press, 2005, p. 56.

TMIY

The Power of God

Emotional Trait	Engaged	Disengaged	Ratio
Feels extremely/very close to father	70	46	1.52
Feels extremely/very close to mother	88	66	1.33
Never feels sad or depressed	23	14	1.64
Never feels alone and misunderstood	39	32	1.22
Feels cared for by guardians	92	73	1.26
Frequently thinks about/plans for the future	87	60	1.45
Never feels like life is meaningless	56	30	1.87

Source: Smith, C., et al., "Soul Searching – The Religious and Spiritual Lives of American Teenagers," Oxford University Press, Oxford, 2005, p. 225 and p. 228.

TMIY

The Power of God

Commandment	Behavior	Engaged	Disengaged	Ratio
Honor parents	Rebellious (parent report)	3	17	5.67
Do not kill	Very bad temper	32	49	1.53
No adultery	Sexual intercourse	9	26	2.89
Do not steal	Cheated on test	6	8	1.33
Do not lie	Frequently lie to parents	4	16	4.00
Do not lust	Internet porn weekly	0	8	**
Do not covet	Don't care about poor	2	6	3.00

Source: Smith, C., et al., "Soul Searching – The Religious and Spiritual Lives of American Teenagers," Oxford University Press, Oxford, 2005, Tables 34-41).

TMIY

Giving Time to Children

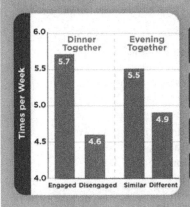

- Children who are engaged in their spiritual lives have parents who spend more time with them than the parents of children who are disengaged.

- Parents of engaged children spend almost one extra afternoon per week with their children compared to parents of disengaged children.

- Parents of engaged children eat an additional dinner every week with their children.

- Parents of engaged children spend an additional 0.6 evenings/week with their children.

Sources: Smith, C., et al., "Soul Searching: The Religious and Spiritual Lives of American Teenagers," Oxford University Press, 2005, p. 226 and p. 228.

TMIY

6-3

The Question of Time

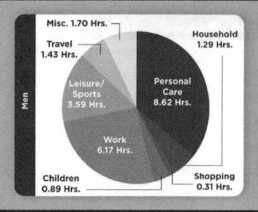

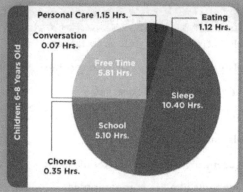

Source: Bureau of Labor Statistics, "American Time Use Survey, Combined Years 2011-2015," Table A-7. (Married Parents, Children under 18 at home, Father data.)

Hofferth, S., "Changes in American children's time - 1997 to 2003," Electronic International Journal of Time Use Research, September 1, 2009, pp. 26-47.

TMIY

The Preventive System of Parenting

> The preventive system consists in making the laws known and then watching carefully so that the pupils may at all times be under the vigilant eye of the Rector, who like loving fathers can... place the pupils in the impossibility of committing faults.
>
> **Don Bosco**

Source: Lemoyne, G., "The Biographical Memoirs of St. John Bosco," v. 4, Salesiana Publishers, Inc., New York, 1967, p. 381.

TMIY

The Presence of the Father

 Don Bosco "was more like a father than a priest, or a teacher."

 "His students... craved his physical presence, the personal relationship."

 Paramount maxim: "For goodness sake, never leave the boys to themselves; keep an eye on them, always and everywhere."

 "The director must be dedicated wholly to the boys entrusted to him and never accept engagements which keep him away from his duties. Rather, he ought to be always with his pupils whenever they are not engaged in some particular occupation, unless they are properly assisted by others."

 Constant companionship with youth is the most demanding of Don Bosco's

Source: Morrison, J., "The Educational Philosophy of St. John Bosco," Salesiana Publishers, New York, 1979.
Lemoyne, G., "The Biographical Memoirs of St. John Bosco," v. 4, Salesiana Publishers, Inc., New York, 1967, p. 382.
Lappin, P., "Give Me Souls: Life of Don Bosco," Salesiana Publishers, New York, 1986.

TMIY

The Path to Joy

Day 1	Avoid travel and entertainment that would draw you away from home.
Day 2	Have dinner with your family at least 5 nights per week.
Day 3	Avoid work or activities on the weekend that take away family time.
Day 4	Check technology at the door until children are in bed.
Day 5	Participate in your children's activities as your entertainment and recreation.
Day 6	Bless your children before bed or whenever they leave the home.

TMIY

SESSION 6

- How important would your wife and children say God is in your life? How has God changed your life?

- How much time do you spend away from your family? How much of it is really necessary? What can you do to spend more time with your family?

Next Week

Week 2: Joyful Service

SESSION 7

Step 2:
Joyful Service

Journey to Joy

Don Bosco: The Festive Oratory ①

Story: Team Hoyt ②

Challenge: Time Crunch ③

Way of Joy: Joyfully Serve ④

Seven Steps

⑤ Find God in Yourself: Presence

⑥ Find God in Other People: Service

⑦ Practice Superabundant Mercy: Sacrifice

① Honor Your Wedding Vows: Purity

② Use Money for Other People: Virtue

③ Give God Some of Your Time: Friends

④ Set Your Mind on Things Above: Wisdom

TMIY

The Challenge of Formation

Human Formation

- Relates to laws of nature and the needs of the material human body.
- Body participates in spiritual reality of person.
- Epigenetics: Behavior changes gene expression.
- Friends and the media have a large influence on behaviors that impact the material body.
- The need for virtue.

Intellectual Formation

- Relates to the brain's desire to know the truth.
- The brain is transformed by experience.
- Feedback loop in reward system either reinforces or avoids behavior for the future.
- The brain anticipates rewards based on past behavior and builds a tolerance for repeated behaviors – building "virtue" or "vice".

Pastoral Formation

- Relates to the communal dimension of the human person and hardwired as a true good.
- Brain uses other brains to organize its own thought processes.
- Mirror neuron system brings other people's actions into our own brain.
- Friends have a large influence.
- Media images condition desire for communion.

Moral Formation

- Relates to human freedom.
- Driven by the brain's reward system.
- Desire to obtain the "good" – determined by hardwiring and experience.
- Conditioned by relationship with God and other people – family and friends; images placed in the brain – especially by the media.

Body · Intellect (Consciousness) · Human Person · Relationships · Will (Freedom)

TMIY

The Experience of the Human Person

- "Early touch experiences determine the extent of possible tactile sensitivity."

- "Familiarity with their mother's scent seems to provide a lot of comfort to young babies... [who] have been observed to slow their often-disorganized body movements in the presence of their mother's scent."

- "Variation in breast milk flavors may play an important role in taste development

- A baby's "vision is also optimized for seeing and learning what her family members look like... Newborns have an innate preference for faces."

- "By birth, babies... have even become somewhat discriminating about what they like to hear. Mother's voice tops the chart."

Source: Eliot, L., "What's Going On In There? How the Brain and Mind Develop in the First Five Years of Life," Bantam Books, New York, 1999.

TMIY

Interpersonal Experience and the Mind

- "At the level of the mind, attachment establishes an interpersonal relationship that helps the immature brain use the mature functions of the parent's brain to organize its own processes."

- Child sends signals regarding its internal state.

- Mother receives child's signals and forms an internal image of the child within herself through the mirror neuron system in the anterior insular cortex.

- Mother signals back, "I have internally aligned with you" and then provides "reality check."

- Child uses mother's contingent communication to organize its own mental processes.

- "Repeated experiences become encoded in implicit memory as expectations and then as mental models."

Sources: Siegel, D., "The Developing Mind: How Relationships and the Brain Interact to Shape Who We Are," 2nd Edition, The Guilford Press, New York, 2012, p. 91. Siegel, Daniel J., et al, "Parenting from the Inside Out," Chapters 2-4, Jeremy P. Tarcher/Penguin, 2003.

TMIY

The Importance of the Father

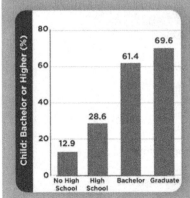

- Controlling for maternal involvement, the presence of the father positively affects cognitive development as early as 6 months.

- Play with father stimulates brain and helps to regulate emotions.

- Quality of relationship with father predicts child's grade point average.

- The educational attainment of children is highly correlated to the educational attainment of their father.

Source: Horn, W., et v, "Father Facts," Fourth Edition, National Fatherhood Initiative, pp. 123-152. General Social Survey, 1972-2012.

TMIY

The Use of Time by 6 to 8 Year Olds

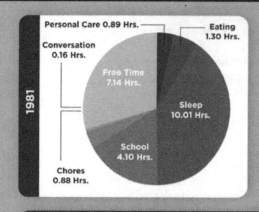
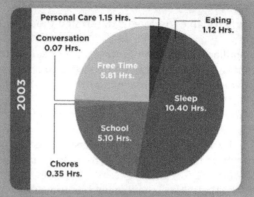

Free time has been reduced almost 10 hours per week. School nights, it has been reduced almost 50%.

Source: Hofferth, S., et al., "Changes in American Children's Time, 1981-1997," Children at the Millennium: Where have We Come from, Where are We Going?, v. 6, pp. 193-229.
Hofferth, S., "Changes in American children's time – 1997 to 2003," Electronic International Journal of Time Use Research, September 1, 2009, pp. 26-47.

TMIY

A Joyful Parenting System

> "
> Let the boys have full liberty to jump, run, and shout as much as they please... 'Do whatever you like,' the great friend of youth, St. Philip Neri, used to say, 'provided that you do not sin.'
>
> **Don Bosco**
> "

Source: Lemoyne, G., "The Biographical Memoirs of St. John Bosco," v. 4, Salesiana Publishers, Inc., New York, 1967, pp. 382-383.

TMIY

Attachment Theory Revisited

Adult Attachment	Child Attachment
Secure/Autonomous Coherent, values attachment	**Secure** Uses parent for secure base.
Dismissing Dismissing of attachment	**Avoidant** Actively avoids parent
Preoccupied Preoccupied with past relationships	**Resistant** Focused on parent without comfort
Disorganized Disorganized thinking (past trauma)	**Disorganized/Disoriented** Disorganized thoughts/behaviors

Source: Siegel, D, "The Developing Mind: Second Edition," The Guilford Press, New York, 2012, pp. 91-45.
Main, M., et al., "Predictability of Attachment Behavior and Representational Processes at 1, 6, and 19 Years of Age," in Attachment from Infancy to Adulthood – The Major Longitudinal Studies," The Guilford Press, New York, 2005, pp. 245-304.

TMIY

The Path to Joy

Day 7	Take time to laugh with your family every day.
Day 8	Take time to play (or have recreation) with your family every week.
Day 9	Do silly things, games or tricks to have fun with your family.
Day 10	When you see a family member at the end of work, ask how their day has been and then listen.
Day 11	Have fun together with your children's friends.
Day 12	Do a "random act of kindness" at least a few times a year for each family member.

TMIY

SESSION 7

THAT MAN IS YOU!

- What was the most fun you have ever had with your child or grandchild? How long ago did it happen? How can you make new memories today?

- How much time do you spend with your family on a daily basis? What do you need to change to spend more?

Next Week

Week 3: Loving Sacrifice

SESSION 8

Step 3:
Loving Sacrifice

Journey to Joy   Seven Steps

Don Bosco: Eucharist and Confession **1**

5 Find God in Yourself: Presence

6 Find God in Other People: Service

Story: Joan and John Pridmore **2**

7 Practice Superabundant Mercy: Sacrifice

Challenge: Abiding Presence - Time **3**

1 Honor Your Wedding Vows: Purity

2 Use Money for Other People: Virtue

Way of Joy: Experience God **4**

3 Give God Some of Your Time: Friends

4 Set Your Mind on Things Above: Wisdom

TMIY

The Challenge of Formation

Human Formation

- Relates to laws of nature and the needs of the material human body.
- Body participates in spiritual reality of person.
- Epigenetics: Behavior changes gene expression.
- Friends and the media have a large influence on behaviors that impact the material body.
- The need for virtue.

Intellectual Formation

- Relates to the brain's desire to know the truth.
- The brain is transformed by experience.
- Feedback loop in reward system either reinforces or avoids behavior for the future.
- The brain anticipates rewards based on past behavior and builds a tolerance for repeated behaviors – building "virtue" or "vice".

Body — Intellect (Consciousness) — Human Person — Relationships — Will (Freedom)

Pastoral Formation

- Relates to the communal dimension of the human person and hardwired as a true good.
- Brain uses other brains to organize its own thought processes.
- Mirror neuron system brings other people's actions into our own brain.
- Friends have a large influence.
- Media images condition desire for communion.

Moral Formation

- Relates to human freedom.
- Driven by the brain's reward system.
- Desire to obtain the "good" – determined by hardwiring and experience.
- Conditioned by relationship with God and other people – family and friends; images placed in the brain – especially by the media.

TMIY

The Physiological Reality for John Pridmore

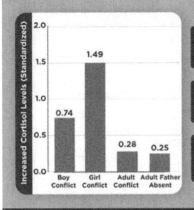

During parent's martial conflict, boy cortisol levels increase by 74%. Girls cortisol levels increase by 149%.

Adults who as children experienced parents with marital conflict have increased cortisol levels.

Adults who as children experienced the absence of their father from the home have increased cortisol levels.

Source: Flinn, M., et al., "Male-Female Differences in Effects of Parental Absence on Glucocorticoid Stress Response," Human Nature, v. 7, No. 2, pp. 125-162, 1996.

TMIY

Industrial Revolution: Father out of Home

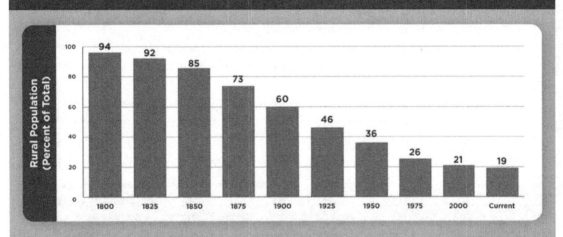

Source: U.S. Department of Commerce, Census Bureau, "Historical Statistics of the United States: Colonial Times to 1970," Part 1, Series A 57-72, pp. 11-12.

TMIY

Information Age: Mothers out of Home

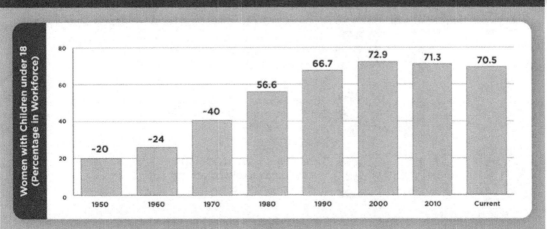

Source: U.S Department of Labor, Bureau of Labor Statistics.
Cohany, R., et al., "Trends in Labor Force Participation of Married Mothers of Infants," Monthly Labor Review,

TMIY

8-2

The Stress of Infants

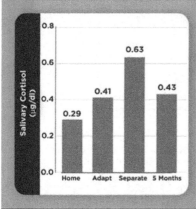

- Approximately seventy percent of mothers with children work outside the home.
- Approximately ¼ of the children of working mothers attend daycare.
- Study of 70 fifteen month old infants introduced to childcare.
- After 5 months, stress hormone levels are approximately 50% above baseline.
- Cortisol levels in children attending daycare increase during the afternoon.

Source: Ahnert, L., et al., "Transition to Child Care: Associations with Infant-Mother Attachment, Infant Negative Emotion, and Cortisol Elevations," Child Development, May/June 2004, v. 75, No. 3, pp. 639–650.

TMIY

The Impact on Attachment

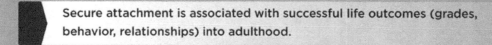

Mother responsiveness to infant needs is a critical component of attachment.
- Breastfeeding leads to more secure attachment.
- Nighttime responsiveness leads to more secure attachment.
- Reduced time in daycare leads to more secure attachment.

Secure attachment is associated with successful life outcomes (grades, behavior, relationships) into adulthood.

Mother stress is a major determinate of mother responsiveness.

Source: Tharner, A., "Breastfeeding and Its Relation to Maternal Sensitivity and Infant Attachment," Journal of Developmental and Behavioral Pediatrics, June 2012, v. 33, no. 5, pp. 396-404.
Higley, E., et al., "Nighttime maternal responsiveness and infant attachment at one year," Attachment Human Development, 2009, July, 11(4): pp. 347-363.
Belsky, J., et al., "Nonmaternal Care in the First Year of Life and the Security of Infant-Parent Attachment," Child Development, v. 59, No, 1, February 1988, pp. 157-167.
Raby, K. L., et al., "The Enduring Predictive Significance of Early Maternal Sensitivity: Social and Academic Competence Through Age 32 Years," Child Development, May/June 2015, v. 86, No. 3, pp. 695-708.
Shin, H., et al., "Maternal sensitivity: a concept analysis," Journal of Advanced Nursing, 2008, 64(3), pp. 304-314.

TMIY

The Experience of God

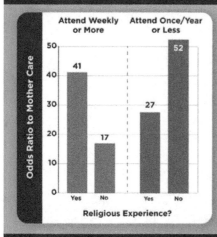

- Approximately 40% of Americans have had a religious experience so profound that it transformed their life.
- Those who have had a religious experience are 2.4 times more likely to attend church services at least weekly.
- Those who have NOT had a religious experience are twice as likely to attend church services once a year or less.

Sources: General Social Survey, 1972-2016.

TMIY

Don Bosco: Making God Tangible

> "Frequent confession and Communion and daily Mass are the pillars which ought to support a system of education from which we wish to banish threats and the whip. Never oblige the boys to frequent the holy sacraments; but only encourage them and give them every opportunity to avail themselves of them."

> "He imbues his boys with such a spirit of piety that he almost inebriates them. The very atmosphere which surrounds them, the air they breathe is impregnated with religion... [The boys] would have to move directly against the current to become bad."

Source: Lemoyne, G., "The Biographical Memoirs of St. John Bosco," v. 4, Salesiana Publishers, Inc., New York, 1967, p. 382.
Lappin, P., "Give Me Souls: Life of Don Bosco," Salesiana Publishers, New York, 1986, p. 149.

TMIY

Experiencing God

Steubenville Youth Conferences

- Over 40,000 youth attend at locations throughout U.S. and Canada.
- Eucharistically focused, dynamic Catholic experience.
- Major source of vocations for the Church.

ND Vision

- Hosted at the University of Notre Dame and facilitated by ND students.
- Liturgically focused and source of vocations for the Church.

Pilgrimage

- Medieval Sites: Holy Land, Rome, Santiago de Compostela.
- Modern Sites: Holy Land, Rome, Lourdes, Fatima.

TMIY

The Path to Joy

Day 13	Destroy the man cave! Don't spend time hanging out alone.
Day 14	Never give up on your children. Pray for them every day.
Day 15	Offer a sacrifice for your children every week.
Day 16	Find something to praise in your child every day.
Day 17	"Punish your own impatience and pride" before correcting your children.
Day 18	Use vacation time to do something to make God tangible to your children.

TMIY

- What is the greatest sacrifice you've ever made for one of your children? What sacrifice are you willing to make to help them now?

- How can you help your children experience God? Have you ever thought of going on a pilgrimage for a family vacation? How about sending your child to a youth conference?

Next Week

Step 4: Purity and Pastoral Formation

SESSION 9

Step 4:
Purity and Pastoral Formation

Journey to Joy   Seven Steps

Don Bosco: Wholesome Arts **1**

Story: Marilyn Monroe **2**

Challenge: The Media **3**

Way of Joy: Devotion to Our Lady **4**

5 Find God in Yourself: Presence

6 Find God in Other People: Service

7 Practice Superabundant Mercy: Sacrifice

1 Honor Your Wedding Vows: Purity

2 Use Money for Other People: Virtue

3 Give God Some of Your Time: Friends

4 Set Your Mind on Things Above: Wisdom

TMIY

Happiness and the 7 Steps

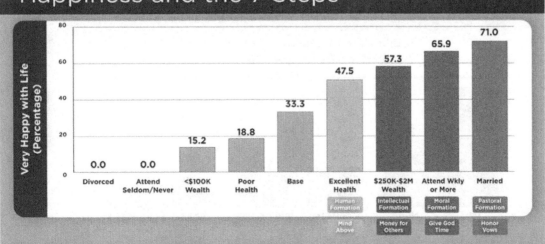

Source: General Social Survey, 1972-2012.

TMIY

The Challenge of Formation

Human Formation
- Nature of the human person: body, soul (mind and will), communion.
- Technology overwhelms mind and will and then isolates.
- "Bad habits"

Intellectual Formation
- Intellect seeks the truth
- Education seeks to form the mind
- Secularized education undermines faith and family
- "Bad books"

Pastoral Formation
- "Man cannot live without love."
- Marriage/family is foundation communion.
- Media undermines faith and family
- "Bad books"

Moral Formation
- Will embraces God as the true good
- Attendance at weekly service
- Friends are a particularly strong influence on faith
- "Bad companions"

Body (Health) — Intellect (Wealth) — Human Person — Relationships (Marriage) — Will (Attendance)

TMIY

Forming a Family

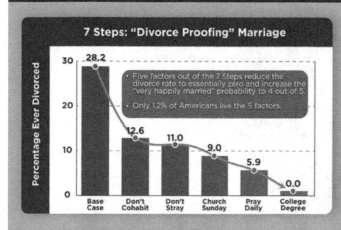

7 Steps: "Divorce Proofing" Marriage

Percentage Ever Divorced

- Base Case: 28.2
- Don't Cohabit: 12.6
- Don't Stray: 11.0
- Church Sunday: 9.0
- Pray Daily: 5.9
- College Degree: 0.0

- Five factors out of the 7 Steps reduce the divorce rate to essentially zero and increase the "very happily married" probability to 4 out of 5.
- Only 1.2% of Americans live the 5 factors.

Millennials and the 5 Factors
- Never married millennials live the 5 Factors at significantly lower levels.
- Do not cohabitate: Approximately 20%
- Pornography(weekly): M-41%; W-19%.
- Attend church weekly: M-13.6%; W-13.0%.
- Pray daily: M-38.5%; W-43.0%.
- College degree: M-27.2%; W-35.0%

Source: Paradisus Dei. General Social Survey, 1972-2016.

TMIY

Media Consumption by Youth

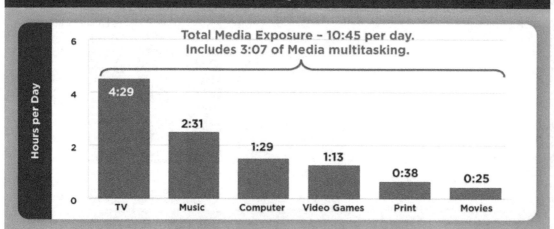

**Total Media Exposure – 10:45 per day.
Includes 3:07 of Media multitasking.**

Hours per Day

- TV: 4:29
- Music: 2:31
- Computer: 1:29
- Video Games: 1:13
- Print: 0:38
- Movies: 0:25

Source: "Generation M2: Media in the Lives of 8 to 18 Year Olds," Kaiser Family Foundation, 2010.

TMIY

Media Depictions of Faith and Family

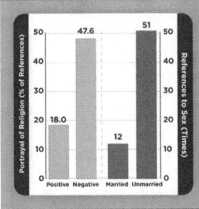

The media has become the primary means of education for faith and relationships.

Formal religious institutions and clearly defined beliefs about God are presented negatively 2.5 times more frequently than positively.

Marriage is most frequently presented as burdensome and confining.

Spoken and visual references to unmarried sex outnumber those to married sex 4.25 to 1 in "Family Hour."

Source: Parents Television Council, "Faith in a Box," December 2006. Parents Television Council, "Happily Never After," August 5, 2008.
Sources: Hjarvard, S., "The Mediatization of Religion," 5th International Conference on Media, Religion, and Culture, Stockholm, 2006.

TMIY

Media Content Changes Religious Behavior

Viewing R-Rated movies decreases church attendance.

Viewing R-Rated movies decreases the importance of faith in the life of the individual.

Parental monitoring/viewing of movie content had a positive impact on religious belief and practice.

"These results suggest that even when controlling for [other variables] viewing R-rated movies still has negative effects on salience of faith and church attendance."

Source: Davignon, R., "The Effects of R-Rated Movies on Adolescent and Young Adult Religiosity: Media and Self-Socialization," Rev Relig Res, 2013, 55, pp. 615-628.

TMIY

Media Content Changes Sexual Behavior

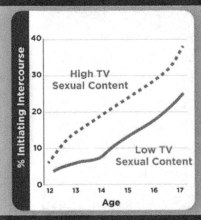

Analyzed TV sexual content consumed by teens and followed up one year later to see sexual experiences.

Higher TV sexual content led to increased sexual activity at all ages.

"In other words, after adjustment for other differences between high and low viewers of sexual content, 12 year-olds who watched the highest levels of this content among youths their age appeared much like youths 2 to 3 years older who watched the lowest levels of sexual content among their peers."

Source: Collins, R., "Watching Sex on Television Predicts Adolescent Initiation of Sexual Behavior," Pediatrics, 2004.

TMIY

Don Bosco and Good Arts

> "The boys were expected to work seriously, but there were compensations. A theatre was one of Don Bosco's earliest enterprises. Plays were acted, historical episodes presented, and music was always to the fore. The choir of the Oratory was in demand for festive occasions all over the city."

> "Ne impedias musicam" (Forbid not music).

> All boarders were required to learn Gregorian chant.

> Don Bosco recited from memory entire sections of the Latin classics (both Church Fathers and secular).

> All boarders required to learn Latin/the Latin classics.

> He used these stories to teach boys valuable moral lessons about life.

Source: Morrison, J., "The Educational Philosophy of St. John Bosco," Salesiana Publishers, New York, 1979, p. 53., 74, 72.

TMIY

The Path to Joy

Day 19	Have your children wear a blessed Miraculous Medal.
Day 20	Avoid all inappropriate media in your own life.
Day 21	Make the sacrifice of your time to have fun with your children.
Day 22	Enjoy appropriate entertainment with your family.
Day 23	Never use the media or technology as "babysitters" or background noise or by default because of boredom.
Day 24	Install filters on all media and technology devices.

TMIY

SESSION 9

THAT MAN IS YOU!

- How much do you use the media - including on your technology? How can you get it under control so that you can enjoy true time with your family? How can you better monitor your children's media consumption?

- How can you unite your children more profoundly to Mary? How can your learn more about her?

Next Week

Week 5: Wealth and Intellectual Formation

SESSION 10

Step 5:
Wealth and Intellectual Formation

Journey to Joy   Seven Steps

Don Bosco: Reason, Religion, Kindness **1**

Story: Howard Storm **2**

Challenge: Secularized Education **3**

Way of Joy: Three Wisdoms **4**

5 Find God in Yourself: Presence

6 Find God in Other People: Service

7 Practice Superabundant Mercy: Sacrifice

1 Honor Your Wedding Vows: Purity

2 Use Money for Other People: Virtue

3 Give God Some of Your Time: Friends

4 Set Your Mind on Things Above: Wisdom

TMIY

The Challenge of Formation

Human Formation

- Nature of the human person: body, soul (mind and will), communion.
- Technology overwhelms mind and will and then isolates.
- "Bad habits"

Intellectual Formation

- Intellect seeks the truth
- Education seeks to form the mind
- Secularized education undermines faith and family
- "Bad books"

Body (Health)

Intellect (Wealth)

Human Person

Relationships (Marriage)

Will (Attendance)

Pastoral Formation

- "Man cannot live without love."
- Marriage/family is foundation communion.
- Media undermines faith and family
- "Bad books"

Moral Formation

- Will embraces God as the true good
- Attendance at weekly service
- Friends are a particularly strong influence on faith
- "Bad companions"

TMIY

The Impact of Education on Wealth

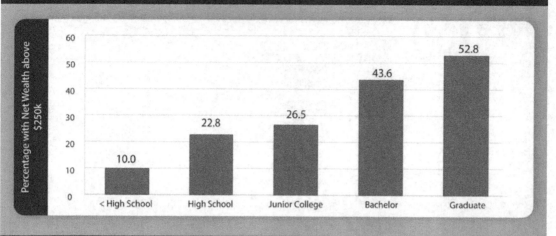

Source: General Social Survey, 2000-2018.

TMIY

The Impact of Education on Faith

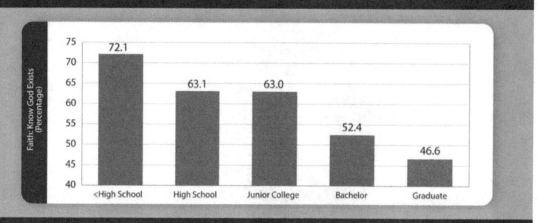

Source: General Social Survey, 2000-2018.

TMIY

The Decline of Reading

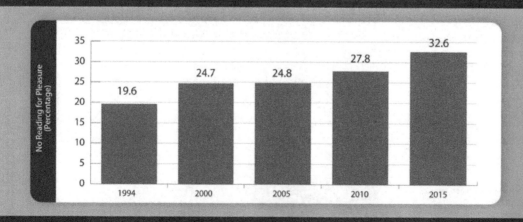

Source: The American Freshman, 50-Year Trends.

TMIY

10-2

Advertising Expenditures: 2021

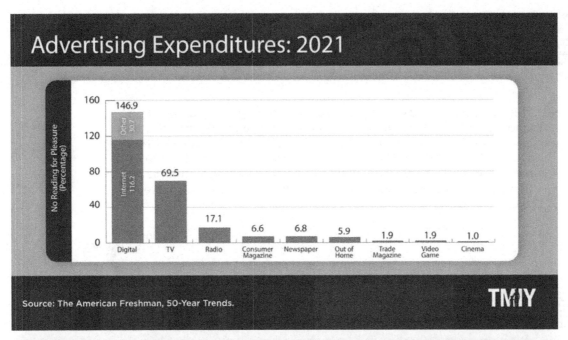

Source: The American Freshman, 50-Year Trends.

TMIY

The Impact of Media Advertising

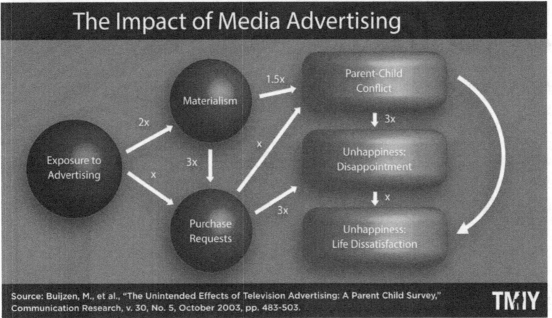

Source: Buijzen, M., et al., "The Unintended Effects of Television Advertising: A Parent Child Survey," Communication Research, v. 30, No. 5, October 2003, pp. 483-503.

TMIY

Wealth and Financial Constraints

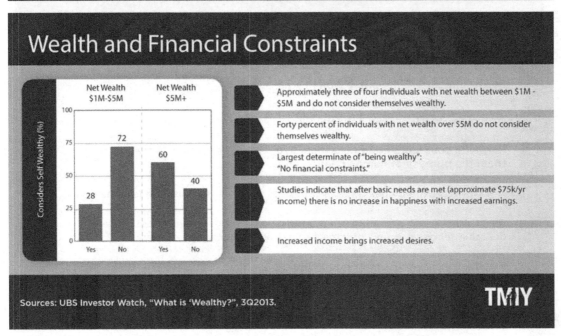

Approximately three of four individuals with net wealth between $1M - $5M and do not consider themselves wealthy.

Forty percent of individuals with net wealth over $5M do not consider themselves wealthy.

Largest determinate of "being wealthy": "No financial constraints."

Studies indicate that after basic needs are met (approximate $75k/yr income) there is no increase in happiness with increased earnings.

Increased income brings increased desires.

Sources: UBS Investor Watch, "What is 'Wealthy?", 3Q2013.

TMIY

A Christian Parenting System

> This system is based entirely on reason and religion, and above on kindness; therefore it excludes all violent punishment, and tries to do without even the slightest chastisement... The practice of this system is based entirely on these words of St. Paul: 'Love is patient, is kind... bears with all things, hopes all things, endures all things... Hence only a Christian can apply the 'Preventive System' with success.
>
> Don Bosco

Source: Lemoyne, G., "The Biographical Memoirs of St. John Bosco," v. 4, Salesiana Publishers, Inc., New York, 1967, pp. 381-382.

TMIY

The Three Wisdoms

"Faith and reason are like two wings upon which the human spirit rises to the contemplation of God" (Pope St. John Paul II, *Fides et Ratio Prologue*).

"The Spirit of the Lord shall rest upon him; the spirit of wisdom and understanding, the spirit of counsel and fortitude, the spirit of knowledge and piety. And his delight shall be in the fear of the Lord" (Isaiah 11:2-3).

Knowledge	Natural knowledge - historically philosophy, especially metaphysics. We use science.
Understanding	Divine revelation based upon Scripture, Tradition and the teachings of the Magisterium.
Wisdom	The contemplative or mystical wisdom the saints enter into.

TMIY

The Path to Joy

Day 25	Study: Integrate faith and reason in your own life.
Day 26	Be a man of virtue: Save $ by avoiding materialism.
Day 27	Play with your children to help them avoid media time and to teach them the primacy of human relationships.
Day 28	Tell stories at the dinner table to integrate faith, reason and life lessons.
Day 29	Teach virtue at the dinner table: never insist on what you want; choose the least desirable item; always say, "best meal I ever had"; help others have joy.
Day 30	Be active in your children's education.

TMIY

SESSION 10

- Do your children/grandchildren attend Catholic or public schools? Is it helping or hindering their faith? Is science causing them to doubt their faith or the teachings of the faith?

- How much media do you and your children consume? How is it in fluencing your desire for material goods? How frequently do material concerns cause tension in the family? How well do you save money?

Next Week

Step 6: Friendships and Moral Formation

Step 6: Friendships and Moral Formation

Journey to Joy

Seven Steps

Don Bosco: The Doorkeeper **1**

Story: Josh Hamilton **2**

Challenge: Bad Companions **3**

Way of Joy: Holy Social Network **4**

5 Find God in Yourself: Presence

6 Find God in Other People: Service

7 Practice Superabundant Mercy: Sacrifice

1 Honor Your Wedding Vows: Purity

2 Use Money for Other People: Virtue

3 Give God Some of Your Time: Friends

4 Set Your Mind on Things Above: Wisdom

TMIY

The Challenge of Formation

Human Formation

- Nature of the human person: body, soul (mind and will), communion.
- Technology overwhelms mind and will and then isolates.
- "Bad habits"

Intellectual Formation

- Intellect seeks the truth
- Education seeks to form the mind
- Secularized education undermines faith and family
- "Bad books"

Pastoral Formation

- "Man cannot live without love."
- Marriage/family is foundation communion.
- Media undermines faith and family
- "Bad books"

Moral Formation

- Will embraces God as the true good
- Attendance at weekly service
- Friends are a particularly strong influence on faith
- "Bad companions"

Body (Health)

Intellect (Wealth)

Relationships (Marriage)

Will (Attendance)

Human Person

TMIY

The Descent of Josh Hamilton

> When I first got into drinking and using drugs, it was because of where I was hanging out, it was who I was hanging out with. You might not do it at first, but eventually, if you keep hanging around long enough, you're going to start doing what they're doing.
>
> Josh Hamilton

Source: Chen, A., Sports Illustrated, "The Super Natural," June 2, 2008.

TMIY

Friends and Substance Abuse

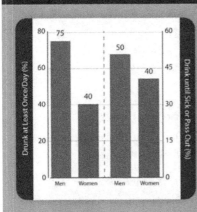

"Peer pressure" strongly influences sexual activity and substance abuse.

Almost 80 percent of college students were introduced to alcohol by their friends.

Almost 95 percent of college students were introduced to drugs by their friends.

Women college students are increasingly adopting risky drinking behaviors to "fit in" and attract men.

Spring Break among college friends.

Source: The National Center on Addiction and Substance Abuse at Columbia University, "Wasting the Best and Brightest: Substance Abuse at America's Colleges and Universities," March 2007, pp. 53-56.

TMIY

Alcohol and Sexual Behavior

Seventy percent of college students admit to having engaged in sexual activity primarily as a result of being under the influence of alcohol.

Seventy-four percent of men and sixty percent of women prefer hooking up when alcohol is involved.

One in twelve college males admit to having committed acts that meet the legal definition of rape or date rape.

Fifty-five percent of female and seventy-five percent of male students involved in date rape admit to having been drinking or using drugs when the incident occurred.

Sixty percent of college women infected with STDs report that they were under the influence of alcohol at the time they had intercourse with the infected person.

Source: http://www.uhs.berkeley.edu/home/healthtopics/sexualassault/saalcohol.shtml.
http://health.iupui.edu/education/drugs/daterape.html.
Bradshaw, C., et al., "To Hook Up or Date: Which Gender Benefits," Sex Roles, 2010,

TMIY

Friends and Faith

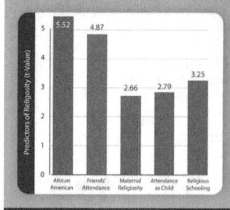

Study following children from youth (age 7-11) to adulthood (age 17-22).

Largest two determinates of religious practice as an adult were being African American and the frequency of friends attending services at age 16.

Impact of friends' religiosity was significantly more important than church attendance as a child, religious schooling and maternal level of religiosity.

Source: Gunnoe, M., et al., "Predictors of Religiosity Among Youth Aged 17-22: A Longitudinal Study of the National Survey of Children," Journal for the Scientific Study of Religion, 41:4, 2002, pp. 613-622.

TMIY

Don Bosco and the Preventive System

"The purpose of this oratory is to keep boys busy and away from bad companions, especially on Sundays and holy days."

"Let the greatest vigilance be exercised so as to prevent bad books, bad companions or persons who indulge in improper conversations from entering the college. A good door-keeper is a treasure for a house of education."

Source: Lemoyne, G., "The Biographical Memoirs of St. John Bosco," v. 3, Salesiana Publishers, Inc., New York, 1966, p. 68. Morrison, J., "The Educational Philosophy of St. John Bosco," Salesiana Publishers, New York, 1979, p. 113.

TMIY

A Climate of Holiness

He imbues his boys with such a spirit of piety that he almost inebriates them. The very atmosphere which surrounds them, the air they breathe is impregnated with religion. The boys... would have to move directly against the current to become bad... Aided by... his spirit of self-sacrifice, his personal sanctity and his charisma, he was able with the passing of time to create... a climate of saints... Sanctity was in the air you breathed. You did not notice its presence so much as its absence the moment you left.

Source: Lappin, P., "Give Me Souls: Life of Don Bosco," Salesiana Publishers, New York, 1986, pp. 149-151.

TMIY

The Impact of Faith and Family on Friendships

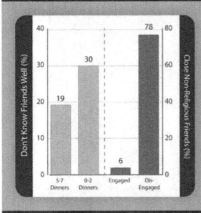

Parents who eat dinner with their children at least 5 nights per week:
- Know their children's friends better.
- Have teens with better relationships with the father and mother.
- Have teens who will confide in them.

- Only 6% of close friendships to teenagers actively engaged in their faith are with nonreligious individuals.
- Approximately 78% of close friendships to teenagers disengaged in their faith are with nonreligious individuals.

Source: Bradshaw, C., et al., "To Hook Up or Date: Which Gender Benefits?" Sex Roles, 2010, 62, pp. 661-669.
Regnerus, M., "Cheap Sex: The Transformation of Men, Marriage, and Monogamy," Oxford University

TMIY

The Path to Joy

Day 31	Establish your social network around individuals of faith - including TMIY.
Day 32	When possible, enroll your children in Catholic schools.
Day 33	Enroll your children in a dynamic Catholic youth program (or start one).
Day 34	Make summer and vacation activities revolve around the faith.
Day 35	Do activities together with your children's friends.
Day 36	Don't be afraid to "interview the date."

TMIY

TMIY
THAT MAN IS YOU!

SESSION 11

- How well do you know your children's friends? How can you get to know them better? What activity could you do with them?

- How do you deal with stress? Do you turn to your pillars of faith and family? How can you teach your children to turn to faith and family when they feel stress?

Next Week

Step 7: Technology and Human Formation

SESSION 12

Step 7:
Technology and
Human Formation

Journey to Joy

Seven Steps

Don Bosco: Nature **1**

Story: Founders of Technology **2**

Challenge: Bad Habits **3**

Way of Joy: Establish JOMO **4**

5 Find God in Yourself: Presence

6 Find God in Other People: Service

7 Practice Superabundant Mercy: Sacrifice

1 Honor Your Wedding Vows: Purity

2 Use Money for Other People: Virtue

3 Give God Some of Your Time: Friends

4 Set Your Mind on Things Above: Wisdom

TMIY

The Challenge of Formation

Human Formation

- Nature of the human person: body, soul (mind and will), communion.
- Technology overwhelms mind and will and then isolates.
- "Bad habits"

Pastoral Formation

- "Man cannot live without love."
- Marriage/family is foundation communion.
- Media undermines faith and family
- "Bad books"

Body
(Health)

Intellect
(Wealth)

Human Person

Relationships
(Marriage)

Will
(Attendance)

Intellectual Formation

- Intellect seeks the truth
- Education seeks to form the mind
- Secularized education undermines faith and family
- "Bad books"

Moral Formation

- Will embraces God as the true good
- Attendance at weekly service
- Friends are a particularly strong influence on faith
- "Bad companions"

TMIY

The Mystery of Technology

> Deep inside every human being there is a source of creativity. A computer should be the extension of the creative human being...
>
> Steve Jobs
>
> We create our technology and then our technology creates us.

Source: Robinson, B., "Appletopia: Media Technology and the Religious Imagination of Steve Jobs," Baylor University Press, 2013, p. 29.

TMIY

Technology Adoption Rates

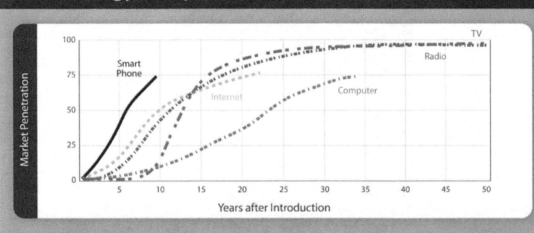

Source: U.S. Department of Commerce, "Computer and Internet Use in the United States: Population Characteristics," May 2013, Figure 1 and September 2017. U.S. Department of Commerce, Census Bureau, "Historical Statistics of the United States: Colonial Times to 1970," Series R 93-105, Series A 288-319. Statistical Abstract of the United States: 2006, Table 1117.

TMIY

Technology in our Lives

- Approximately 75% of youth have a smartphone.
- High School students spend over 5 hours per day on their smartphone.
- Almost half of teens feel addicted to their smartphone.
- Approximately 78% of youth check their smartphone at least hourly.
- One-third of parents argue with their children on a daily basis about their usage of a smartphone.
- Seventy-seven percent of parents feel their children are distracted during personal time together because of their smartphone.
- Approximately 84% of youth use social media. Almost 2 out of 3 youth check their social media site daily.
- The average youth sends 1800 text messages a month. It is the dominant means of communication.

Source: USC Annenberg/common sense, "The New Normal: Parents, Teens and Digital Devices in Japan," 2017.
Pew Research, "Teens and Technology 2013," March 13, 2013.
Pew Research, "Social Media Update 2013," December 30, 2013.
Pew Research, "Teens, Smartphones & Texting," March 19, 2012.

TMIY

Becoming a "Micro-Celebrity"

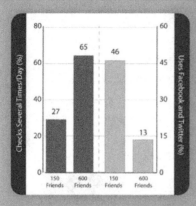

- Technology is an integral part of teen women's social networking.
- Teen girls send almost 4000 messages/month.
- Seventy-six percent of women use Facebook; of those, 3 of 4 visit the site at least daily.
- Teens actively manage accounts "like Madison Avenue" to gain social standing - i.e. to gain "likes."
- "Authenticity is not valued on Facebook. It's not about being authentic. It's about being cool."
- "Every young person has become… a public figure. And so they have adopted the skills that celebrities learn in order not to go crazy."

Sources: Pew Research, "Teens, Social Media, and Privacy," May 21, 2013. Sax, L., "Girls on the Edge," Basic Books, New York, 2010, p. 39 and p. 65.

TMIY

Playing to the Male Audience

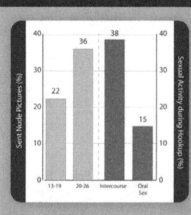

- A large portion of teen and young women text nude or semi-nude pictures of themselves.
- Almost half of young women say that it is common for pictures to be shared with other people.
- Many women admit to being more sexually forward through technology than in "real life."
- Many women admit that sexting makes it more likely to hookup.
- Seventy-six percent of college students will have at least 1 hookup.

Sources: The National Campaign to Prevent Teen and Unplanned Pregnancy, "Sex and Tech: Results from a Survey of Teens and Young Adults," 2008.
England, P., et al., "Hookup and Forming Romantic Relationships on Today's College Campuses," The Gendered Society Reader, Oxford University Press, 5th Edition, 2013.

TMIY

A Failed Proposition

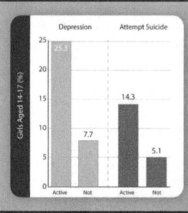

- During physical intimacy, the hormone oxytocin is released.
- Oxytocin neurochemically wires the brain for trust and intimacy.
- Neurological pathways are strengthened, making future sexual activity more likely.
- Destruction of a relationship destroys feelings of intimacy and trust.
- Sexual activity is associated with increased levels of depression and attempted suicide, especially for women.

Source: Rector, R., "Sexually Active Teenagers are More Likely to be Depressed and to Attempt Suicide," The Heritage Foundations, 2003.

TMIY

Boys, the Internet and Pornography

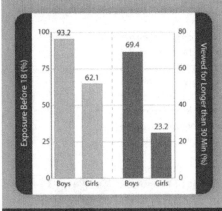

Over ninety percent of boys and sixty percent of girls aged 18 have been exposed to internet pornography.

Boys are three times more likely to seek out pornography to view.

Forty-six percent of men under age 40 view pornography every week.

Almost ¼ of men view pornography on a daily basis.

Pornography mimics a real sexual encounter in the brain.

Sources: Sabina, C., Et al., "The Nature and Dynamics of Internet Pornography Exposure for Youth," CyberPsychology & Behavior, v., 11, No. 6, 2008, Table 1.
Robinson, M., et al, "Cupid's Poisoned Arrow – Porn-Induced Sexual Dysfunction: A Growing Problem," Psychology Today, July 11, 2011.

TMIY

Losing Interest in Sex

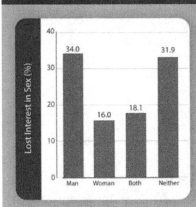

Processed like cocaine, dopamine is implicated in all addictions since the brain develops increased tolerance.

Dopamine activates the sexual centers in the hypothalamus, which sends signals to the erection center in the spinal cord, which sends signals to cause an erection.

Pornography consumption leads to erectile dysfunction and the loss of interest in sex with a real person.

Estimated that 1/3 of people in their early 20's will never marry.

Source: Robinson, M., et al, "Cupid's Poisoned Arrow – Porn-Induced Sexual Dysfunction: A Growing Problem," Psychology Today, July 11, 2011.
Schneider, J., "Effects of Cybersex Addiction on the Family: Results of a Survey," Sexual Addiction and Compulsivity, 2000.

TMIY

The Reward System and Technology

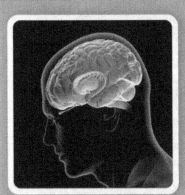

Caudate Nucleus: Identifies and distinguishes between rewards.

Ventral Tegmental Area (VTA): Produces dopamine.

Nucleus Accumbens: Releases dopamine.

The brain seeks information and social connection as a reward.

Informational email and texts are particularly attractive because they are personal.

The brain anticipates a dopamine reward with every "ding" or new friend.

"Friends" and "likes" on social media are perceived as "victories" or "rewards."

Sources: Coates, J., "The Hour Between Dog and Wolf," Penguin Books, 2012.

TMIY

Imitating Reality

> God only knows what it's doing to our children's brains. The thought process that went into building these applications, Facebook being the first of them... was all about, "How do we consume as much of your time and conscious attention as possible?" And that means that we need to sort of give you a little dopamine hit every once in a while, because someone liked or commented on a photo or a post or whatever... It's a social-validation feedback loop... Exactly the kind of thing that a hacker like myself would come up with, because you're exploiting a vulnerability in human psychology. The inventors, creators... understood this consciously. And we did it anyway.
>
> **Sean Parker**
> **First President of Facebook**

TMIY

The Path to Joy

Day 37	Create JOMO opportunities (the Joy of Missing Out).
Day 38	Enjoy nature together with your family as much as possible.
Day 39	Use the Liturgical Calendar of the Church to establish Feast Days to bring joy into your family - especially Christmas, Easter, and feast days of Our Lady and St. Joseph.
Day 40	Establish "family feast days" - especially anniversaries and birthdays.

TMIY

 **SESSION 12**

THAT MAN IS YOU!

- How much time do you spend on your mobile phone every day? Do you use it when you're in the presence of someone else?

- How much time do your children spend on mobile technology? Are the addicted? How can you guard them regarding technology like you would another addiction?

Next Week

The Light of Love

SESSION 13

The Light of Love

The Challenge of Formation

Human Formation

- Nature of the human person: body, soul (mind and will), communion.
- Technology overwhelms mind and will and then isolates.
- "Bad habits"

Intellectual Formation

- Intellect seeks the truth
- Education seeks to form the mind
- Secularized education undermines faith and family
- "Bad books"

Pastoral Formation

- "Man cannot live without love."
- Marriage/family is foundation communion.
- Media undermines faith and family
- "Bad books"

Moral Formation

- Will embraces God as the true good
- Attendance at weekly service
- Friends are a particularly strong influence on faith
- "Bad companions"

Body (Health) · Intellect (Wealth) · Relationships (Marriage) · Will (Attendance) · Human Person

TMIY

Parents, Dinner and Technology

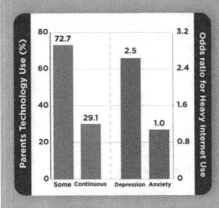

- Almost ¾ of parents use their mobile technology while eating out with their children.
- Approximately thirty percent use it continuously while ignoring the child.
- Majority of children seek to gain their parent's attention, which isn't given.
- Five percent of parents give their children technology to pacify.
- Frequent to compulsive use of the internet is associated with a 2.5 times increase risk of depression.

Sources: Radesky, J., et al., "Patterns of Mobile Device Use by Caregivers and Children During Meals in Fast Food Restaurants," Pediatrics, March 10, 2014.
Lam, L., et al., "Effect of Pathological Use of the Internet on Adolescent Mental Health," Archives of Pediatric Adolescent Medicine, August 2, 2010.

TMIY

Technology and the Brain

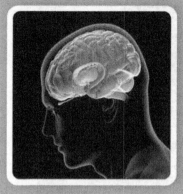

Violent video games: 10 hours of a violent video game altered brain activity in the left inferior front lobe and the anterior cingulate cortex.

These regions are important for cognitive function and emotional control.

Within five hours of internet use, first time internet users are able to activate regions of their brain (dorso-lateral prefrontal cortex) mirroring the brain function of experienced internet users.

Source: Wang, Y., "Violent Video Games Alter Brain Function in Young Men," Annual Meeting of the Radiological Society of North America, 2011.
Small, G., et al., iBrain: Surviving the Technological Alteration of the Modern Mind," William Morrow Paperbacks, 2009, pp. 16-17.

TMIY

The Internet and the Brain

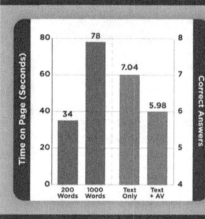

Of its nature, the internet alters the way the brain processes information.

Individuals skim information as they move from page to page.

Prefrontal cortex works at elevated levels to sort through information.

Working memory is overwhelmed.

"Consolidation" into long-term memory doesn't happen lessening the brain's ability to reflect.

The brain accepts what it receives, which is based on popularity.

Sources: Nielsen, J., "How Little Do Users Read?," Alertbox, May 6, 2008.
Rockwell, S., et al., "The Effect of the Modality of Presentation of Streaming Multimedia on Information Acquisition," Media Psychology, 9, pp. 179-191, 2007.

TMIY

The Preferred Solution: Medication

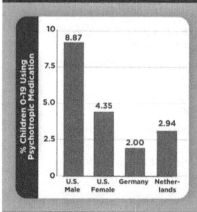

When children seek attention or become "difficult" be-cause of the demands, many are placed on medications.

Prescriptions for psychotropic medications increased 30 times between 1987 and 2007.

Boys are twice as likely as girls to be prescribed medicine for ADHD.

American youth are 3 times more likely to be taking psycho-tropic medicine than youth in Germany or the Netherlands.

Psychotropic medicines effect the nucleus accumbens, which regulates motivation.

Source: Zito, J., et al., "A three-country comparison of psychotropic medication prevalence in youth," Child and Adolescent Psychiatry and Mental Health, September 25, 2008.
Sax, L., "Boys Adrift," Basic Books, New York, 2007, pp. 79-97.

TMIY

The Reality for Children: Take 1

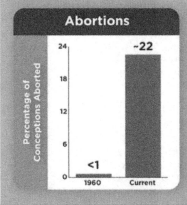

Source: Statistical Abstract of the U.S.
Source: Statistical Abstract of the US., Vital Statistics of the US.
Source: The Religious Factor," (Lenkski, G., 1961). "The Number, Timing and Durantion of Marriages and Divorce: 1996," U.S. Census Bureau.

TMIY

The Reality for Children: Take 2

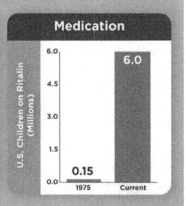

Source: Cohany, R., et al., "Trends in Labor Force Participation of Married Mothers of Infants," Monthly Labor Review, February 2007.
Source: Hofferth, S., et al., "Changes in American Children's Time, 1981-1997" and"Changes in American children's time – 1997 to 2003."
Source: Sax, L., "Ritalin: Better living through chemistry?, " The World and I, November 2000.

TMIY

The Singularity is Near

 "The next step in this inexorable evolutionary process: the union of human and machine, in which the knowledge and skills embedded in our brains will be combined with the vastly greater capacity, speed and knowl-edge-sharing ability of our own creations."

 "Our intelligence will become increasingly nonbiological and trillions of times more powerful."

 We "will be able to transcend our biological limitations... there will be no clear distinction between human and machine... we will be able to assume different bodies and take on a range of personae at will."

Source: Singularity.com discussing Kurzweil, R., "The Singularity is Near: When Humans Transcend Biology," Penguin Books, 2005.

TMIY

Moving Beyond Human Interaction

Several societies are seeking ways to provide for the growing number of elderly, who frequently do not have ongoing family relationships.

"Robot therapy" is advancing in cultures with a rapidly aging population: "human-interactive robots for psychological enrichment, which provide services by interacting with humans while stimulating their minds, are rapidly spreading."

"In robot therapy, it is important to stimulate people's knowledge and experiences of animals through interaction with the robots and to bring out their feelings."

"The next generation will become accustomed to a range of relationships: some with pets, others with people, some with avatars, some with computer agents on screens, and still others with robots. Confiding in a robot will be just one among many choices. We will certainly make our peace with the idea that grandchildren and great grandchildren may be too jumpy to be the most suitable company for their elders."

Source: Shibata, T., et al., "Robot Therapy: A New Approach for Mental Healthcare of the Elderly – a Mini-Review," Gerontology, 2011.
Turkle, S., "Alone Together – Why We Expect more from Technology and Less from Each Other," Basic Books, New York, 2011.

TMIY

The Importance of the Family

"Tell all the congregation of Israel that on the tenth day of this month they shall take every man a lamb according to their fathers' houses, a lamb for a household... This day shall be for you a memorial day, and you shall keep it as a feast to the LORD; throughout your generations... when your children say to you, 'What do you mean by this service?' you shall say, 'It is the sacrifice of the LORD'S passover, for he passed over the houses of the people of Israel in Egypt, when he slew the Egyptians'" (Exodus 12:3-27).

"And day by day, attending the temple together and breaking bread in their homes... praising God and having favor with all the people. And the Lord added to their number day by day those who were being saved" (Acts 2:46-47).

TMIY

Finding Christ at the Dinner Table

" Two of them were going to a village named Emmaus... while they were talking and discussing together, Jesus himself drew near and went with them... And he said to them, 'What is this conversation which you are holding with each other as you walk?'... And beginning with Moses and all the prophets, he interpreted to them in all the scriptures the things concerning himself... They constrained him, saying, 'Stay with us'... When he was at table with them, he took the bread and blessed, and broke it, and gave it to them. And their eyes were opened and they recognized him.

Luke 24:13-31 "

TMIY

The Liturgy of the Table

1. Accompaniment in daily life
- Requires presence (Faucauld).
- Requires time.

2. Questions about everyday life
- Requires listening.

3. The Word of God
- Clarity about one's life is discovered in the truth of the Scriptures.

4. The Discovery of God
- Christ is discovered in communion at the table.

The Liturgy of the Home

Celebrate the major feast days of the Church with great joy:
Easter, Christmas and Pentecost.

Celebrate the feast days of Our Lady and St. Joseph.

Let every member of your family choose his or her favorite feast days to celebrate.

Celebrate "family feast days":
- Wedding Anniversary (which is like an ecclesia domestica Pentecost):
  "Send down on them the grace of the Holy Spirit and pour your love into their hearts" (Nuptial Blessing).
- Birthdays (which are like ecclesia domestica Christmas):
  "By his Incarnation the Son of God has united himself in some fashion with every man" (Vatican II, Gaudium et Spes, #22).
- Other special days in the life of the family.

Living the Festive Oratory

Abiding Presence — Be truly present to your family... especially at dinner, on weekends and "feast days."

Joyful Service — Have fun with your family. The Festive Oratory was a lot of fun for the boys... and exhausting for Don Bosco.

Loving Sacrifice — Sacrifice your other desires to truly have time with your family. Check your phone at the door when you get home so that you're mentally present as well as physically present.

- What is the most important insight you gained this Fall regarding forming children? What is the most tangible step you are going to take to form children?

- How are you going to get control of technology for yourself? For your children?

January

Building a Culture of Peace

SESSION 14

Building a Culture of Peace

The Four Leadership Roles of Men

Political Leadership — Harmoniously order society to peace.

Moral Leadership — Live in union with God to receive His blessings.

Men's Leadership Roles

Economic Leadership — Make the earth fruitful, which is tied to the fruitfulness of the womb.

Military Leadership — Battle Satan over the family, the channel of grace.

TMIY

A Sustainable Socioeconomic Model

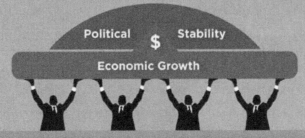

Political $ Stability

Economic Growth

Human Capital Formation - Family & Formal Education

God

TMIY

A Moment Outside of Time

 It was then that I witnessed for the first time something I will truly never forget... His head was bowed and he was absorbed in prayer, totally immobile, without even the slightest movement. He was in a sort of trance – or I dare say, ecstasy... The unreal sparkle of the snow all around emphasized this impression. A complete silence descended... There was no flapping of a wing or the call of a bird, no gentle impact of clumps of snow falling to ground... I know that setting well – the peaks, the glaciers. I have spent much of my life in places like that, and I know that the silence of the mountain is full of voices, sounds, animal cries, the wind itself. At that moment, however, everything seemed to have stopped, truly everything. As if under a spell... I saw how a normal man can cross the boundary and emanate sanctity. **"**

Source: Zani, L., "The Secret Life of John Paul II," Saint Benedict Press, Charolette, NC, 2012.

TMIY

A Vision Through Time

 Pope [John Paul II] does indeed cherish a great expectation that the millennium of divisions will be followed by a millennium of unifications. He has in some sense the vision that the first Christian millennium was the millennium of Christian unity; ... the second millennium was the millennium of great divisions; and that now, precisely at the end, we could rediscover a new unity.

Joseph Cardinal Ratzinger
The Salt of the Earth

"

Source: Zani, L., Joseph Cardinal Ratzinger (with Peter Seewald), The Salt of the Earth," Ignatius Press, San Francisco, 1997, p. 237.

TMIY

The Climactic Confrontation

The world is facing "the greatest historical confrontation humanity has gone through ... the final confrontation between the Church and the anti-Church, or the Gospel versus the anti-Gospel."

"In our times evil has grown disproportionately, operating through perverted systems which have practiced violence and elimination on a vast scale... The evil of the twentieth century was not a small-scale evil, it was not simply 'homemade.' It was an evil of gigantic proportions."

Source: Wojtyla, K., quoted in Wall Street Journal, November 9, 1978. Pope John Paul II, "Memory and Identity," Rizzoli, New York, 2005, p. 167.

14-2

The Lines of Battle

The family is placed at the heart of the great struggle between good and evil, between life and death, between love and all that is opposed to love.

Pope John Paul II
Letter to Families, #23

TMIY

Hope for Tomorrow

This time, in which God in His hidden design has entrusted to me... the universal service connected with the Chair of St. Peter in Rome, is already very close to the year 2000... We also are in a certain way in a season of new Advent, a season of new expectation.

Redemptor Hominis #1

TMIY

A New Springtime for Christianity

Now is the time for hope... We must not be afraid of the future. We must not be afraid of man... Each and every human person has been created in the 'image and likeness' of the One who is the origin of all that is... with the help of God's grace, we can build in the next century and the next millennium a civilization worthy of the human person... And in doing so, we shall see that the tears of this century have prepared the ground for a new springtime of the human spirit.

Pope John Paul II
Address to the United Nations
October 5, 1995

TMIY

SESSION 14

- What do you know about Pope St. John Paul II's vision for the Church?

- When have you had a moment when you were most transformed by prayer?

Next Week

A Novena in Nazareth

A Novena in Nazareth

The Vision of Pope John Paul II

"In our times evil has grown disproportionately, operating through perverted systems which have practiced violence and elimination on a vast scale... The evil of the twentieth century was not a small-scale evil, it was not simply 'homemade.' It was an evil of gigantic proportions."

"I see the dawning of a new missionary age, which will become a radiant day bearing an abundant harvest... As the third millennium of the redemption draws near, God is preparing a great springtime for Christianity" (Pope John Paul II, Redemptoris Missio, #92 and #86).

Source: Pope John Paul II, "Memory and Identity," Rizzoli, New York, 2005, p. 167.

TMIY

A "New Pentecost"

"Renew in our own days your miracles as of a second Pentecost" (Pope St. John XXIII, Preparatory Prayer for Vatican II).

"Christ whom we have contemplated and loved bids us to set out once more on our journey... and urges us to share the enthusiasm of the very first Christians: we can count on the power of the same Spirit who was poured out at Pentecost and who impels us still today to start out anew, sustained by the hope 'which does not disappoint'" (Pope St. John Paul II, *Novo Millennio Ineunte, #58*).

TMIY

The Mystery of Nazareth

Pope St. John XXIII visits the Holy House at Loreto, Italy on October 4, 1962 to entrust the Second Vatican Council to Our Lady: "Today, in the name of the entire episcopate, I ask you, sweetest mother... to intercede for me as Bishop of Rome and for all the bishops of the world, to obtain for us the grace to enter the Council Hall of Saint Peter's Bascilica, as the Apostles and first disciples of Jesus entered the Upper Room" (Pope St. John XXIII, October 4, 1962).

Pope St. John Paul II's last trip outside of Italy was to Lourdes, France.

Pope St. John Paul II's last trip outside of Rome was to Loreto, Italy: "Just as Jesus needed Mary's fiat to become flesh, so his Gospel also needs your 'yes' in order to become history in the contemporary world... Dear Friends, I invite you to renew your 'yes' and I consign to you three duties: the first is 'contemplation'... The second duty is 'communion'... The third duty is 'mission'... May the sweet Lady of Loreto obtain for you fidelity to your vocation" (Pope St. John Paul II, September 5, 2004).

TMIY

The Gift of the Holy Spirit

"The Holy Spirit will come upon you, and the power of the Most High will overshadow you; therefore the child to be born will be called holy, the Son of God" (Luke 1:35).

"All of these with one accord devoted themselves to prayer, together with the women and Mary the mother of Jesus... When the day of Pentecost had come, they were all together in one place. And suddenly a sound came from heaven like the rush of a mighty wind, and it filled all the house where they were sitting. And there appeared to them tongues as of fire, distributed and resting on each one of them. And they were all filled with the Holy Spirit and began to speak in other tongues, as the Spirit gave them utterance" (Acts 1:14; 2:1-4).

"When the Holy Spirit... finds Mary in a soul, he hastens there and enters fully into it. He gives himself generously to the soul according to the place it has give to his spouse [Mary]" (St. Louis de Montfort).

Source: St. Louis de Montfort, "True Devotion to Mary," #36, quoted in "God Alone: The Collected Writings of St. Louis Marie de Montfort," Montfort Publications, Bay Shore, NY, 1987, p. 299.

TMIY

The Importance of the Holy Family

"In this great undertaking, which is the renewal of all things in Christ, marriage... becomes a new reality... We see that at the beginning of the New Testament, as at the beginning of the Old, there is a married couple. But whereas Adam and Eve were the source of evil which was unleashed on the world, Joseph and Mary are the summit from which holiness spreads over all the earth."

Pope St. John Paul II
Redemptoris Custos, #7

TMIY

The Mystery of Paradise

The Garden of Eden	Agony in the Garden	Resurrection in the Garden	The Eschatological Garden

The Temple

The Church

The Holy Family

"The LORD God planted a garden in Eden, in the east" (Genesis 2:8).

"There was a garden, which he and his disciples entered" (John 18:1).

"In the place where he was crucified there was a garden" (John 19:41).

"Then he showed me... the tree of life" (Revelation 22:1-2).

TMIY

A Novena in Nazareth

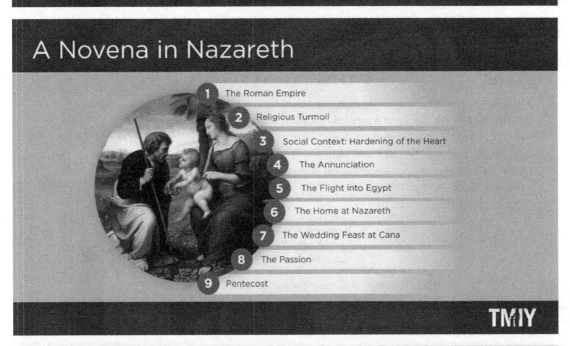

1. The Roman Empire
2. Religious Turmoil
3. Social Context: Hardening of the Heart
4. The Annunciation
5. The Flight into Egypt
6. The Home at Nazareth
7. The Wedding Feast at Cana
8. The Passion
9. Pentecost

TMIY

Mercy as the Light to Our Path

" The light of divine mercy will illumine the way for the men and women of the third millennium... this consoling message is addressed above all to those who, afflicted by a particularly harsh trial or crushed by the weight of the sins they committed, have lost all confidence in life and are tempted to give in to despair.

Pope St. John Paul II "

TMIY

Weekly Plan

A Novena in Nazareth

Apply experience of Holy Family to today. **1**

Consider the response of St. Joseph. **2**

Paradisus Dei New Springtime Prayer **3**

Divine Mercy Chaplet **4**

Listen to the voice of the Holy Spirit. **5**

List how our family is impacted. **6**

List plan of action. **7**

1 The Roman Empire

2 Religious Turmoil

3 Social Context: Hardening of the Heart

4 The Annunciation

5 The Flight into Egypt

6 The Home at Nazareth

7 The Wedding Feast at Cana

8 The Passion

9 Pentecost

TMIY

Building the New Springtime

 The aspiration that humanity nurtures, amid countless injustices and sufferings, is the hope of a new civilization marked by freedom and peace. But for such an undertaking, a new generation of builders is needed... You are the men and women of tomorrow. The future is in your hearts and in your hands. God is entrusting to you the task, at once difficult and uplifting, of working with him in the building of the civilization of love.

Pope St. John Paul II
Evening Vigil with Young People, #4
World Youth Day, Toronto, 2002
Downsview Park, Saturday 27, 2002

TMIY

TMIY SESSION 15

THAT MAN IS YOU

- In what ways is your family being impacted by the current culture? For good? For bad?

- How does God want to use you to help build a better culture for the next generation? Are you open to his call?

Next Week

The 1st Day:
The Roman Empire

SESSION 16

The 1st Day:
The Roman Empire

Weekly Plan

1. Apply experience of Holy Family to today.
2. Consider the response of St. Joseph.
3. Paradisus Dei New Springtime Prayer
4. Divine Mercy Chaplet
5. Listen to the voice of the Holy Spirit.
6. List how our family is impacted.
7. List plan of action.

A Novena in Nazareth

1. The Roman Empire
2. Religious Turmoil
3. Social Context: Hardening of the Heart
4. The Annunciation
5. The Flight into Egypt
6. The Home at Nazareth
7. The Wedding Feast at Cana
8. The Passion
9. Pentecost

TMIY

The Holy Family and the Power of Rome

> "In those days a decree went out from Caesar Augustus that all the world should be enrolled… And all went to be enrolled, each to his own city. And Joseph also went up from Galilee, from the city of Nazareth, to Judea, to the city of David, which is called Bethlehem, because he was of the house and lineage of David, to be enrolled with Mary, his betrothed, who was with child."
>
> **Luke 2:1-5**

TMIY

The Dragon and the First Beast

 "Another portent appeared in heaven; behold, a great red dragon, with seven heads and ten horns, and seven diadems upon his heads" (Revelation 12:3).

 "And I saw a beast rising out of the sea, with ten horns and seven heads, with ten diadems upon its horns and a blasphemous name upon its heads... And to it the dragon gave his power and his throne and great authority... Also it was allowed to make war on the saints and to conquer them" (Revelation 13:1-7).

 "This calls for a mind with wisdom: the seven heads... are also seven kings, five of whom have fallen, one is, the other has not yet come" (Revelation 17:9-10).

TMIY

The Mystery of Paradise

The Garden of Eden	Agony in the Garden	Resurrection in the Garden	The Eschatological Garden

The Temple

The Church

The Holy Family

"The LORD God planted a garden in Eden, in the east" (Genesis 2:8).

"There was a garden, which he and his disciples entered" (John 18:1).

"In the place where he was crucified there was a garden" (John 19:41).

"Then he showed me... the tree of life" (Revelation 22:1-2).

TMIY

The Age of the Church

 "The Old Testament comprises two times: before the Law, and under the Law. In the New Testament, likewise, there are two corresponding times: the time of the calling of the Gentiles that corresponds to the first, and the time of the calling of the Jews that corresponds to the second. This time is not yet, for then will be fulfilled these words of Isaiah: 'One nation shall not raise the sword against another, nor shall they train for war again' (Isaiah 2:4). For this is not yet fulfilled since... there are still disputes and heresies. Hence the Jews, who are waiting for this [the coming of the time of peace] believe Christ has not yet come" (15:24).

 "Lest you be wise in your own conceits, I want you to understand this mystery, brethren: a hardening has come upon part of Israel, until the full number of the Gentiles come in, and so all Israel will be saved" (Romans 11:25-26).

 "It is certain that ... peace will be given. But first, tribulation must come to pass" (16.19).

Source: Bonaventure, Collationes in Hexaemeron, The Works of Bonaventure, v. 5, St. Anthony Guild Press.

TMIY

The "Vision" of Pope St. John Paul II

"Ricoeur has called Freud, Marx, and Nietzsche 'masters of suspicion,' having in mind the whole system each one represents... the thinkers mentioned above... have exercised and still exercise a great influence on the way of thinking and evaluating people of our time" (Wednesday Audience, October 29, 1980).

"It is legitimate and even necessary to ask whether [the culture of the West] is not the work of another ideology of evil, more subtle and hidden, perhaps, intent upon exploiting human rights themselves against man and against the family" (*Memory and Identity, p. 11*).

TMIY

Original Sin as the Template

"This is truly the key for interpreting reality... Original sin attempts, then, to abolish fatherhood" (Pope John Paul II, *Crossing the Threshold of Hope*).

"The serpent was more subtle than any other wild creature that the Lord God had made. He said to the woman, 'Did God say, `You shall not eat of any tree of the garden?`... You will not die. For God knows that when you eat of it your eyes will be opened, and you will be like God, knowing good and evil' (Genesis 3:1-5).

"And the eyes of them both were opened: and when they perceived themselves to be naked, they sewed together fig leaves, and made themselves clothes. And when they heard the voice of the Lord God walking in paradise at the afternoon air, Adam and his wife hid themselves from the face of the Lord God amidst the trees of paradise" (Genesis 3:7-8).

TMIY

 So the first sin may not only be considered as a purely formal one of disobedience of God. Rather it implied a definitive act which had been forbidden and which the serpent presented enticingly to the woman and then the woman to the man. Indeed, the act committed could well have been a manner of union which was at variance with the original order. But that the tempter first tempted the woman may signify... [that] the nature of the temptation was in itself of greater significance for her. From the first it was intended that woman's life would be more strongly affected by procreation and the education of posterity.

St. Edith Stein

Source: Stein, E., "Woman," The Collected Works of Edith Stein, Volume II, Translated Oben, F. M., ICS Publications, Washington DC, 1996, p. 64.

TMIY

The Legal Dismantling of Christian Culture

1960	FDA approves Birth Control Pill
1962	Engel v. Vitale – Prayer in School
1965	Griswold v. Connecticut – Contraception
1966	Memoirs v. Massachusetts – Obscene Material
1969	California Family Law Act – "No Fault Divorce"
1973	Miller v. California – Pornography
1973	Roe v. Wade – Abortion
1996	Romer v. Evans – Sexual Orientation Protected Class
2002	Ashcroft v. Free Speech Coalition/ACLU – "Child Online Protection Act" Unconstitutional.
2015	Obergefell v. Hodges – Gay Marriage

TMIY

"Agenda for Women's Empowerment"

> The Platform for Action is an agenda for women's empowerment. It aims... at removing all the obstacles to women's active participation in all spheres of public and private life through a full and equal share in economic, social, cultural and political decision-making... Maternity, motherhood, parenting and the role of women in procreation must not be a basis for discrimination nor restrict the full participation of women in society.
>
> **United Nations 4th World Conference on Women**
> **Beijing, China, September 4-15, 1995**
> *Conference Report, #1, #29*

TMIY

The Ultimate Market

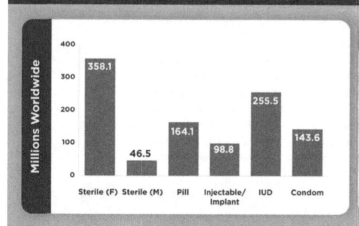

Bar chart — Millions Worldwide:
- Sterile (F): 358.1
- Sterile (M): 46.5
- Pill: 164.1
- Injectable/Implant: 98.8
- IUD: 255.5
- Condom: 143.6

Region	% Modern*
Western Europe	66.8
Australia/New Zealand	65.6
Northern Europe	73.4
North America	69.3
Central America	65.5
Eastern Asia	80.4
Middle Africa	11.0
Eastern Africa	35.9

Source: United Nations, Trends in Contraception Use Worldwide, 2015. United Nations Population Division, World Population Prospects 2017, Female Population by 5-year age groups 15-49.
Source: Percentage of women aged 15-49, in a union. United Nations Population Division, World Contraceptive Use, 2015.
*Includes: Sterilization, Pill, Injectable, Implant, IUD, Condom, Vaginal Barrier.

TMIY

Fertility Change in the Life of the Couple

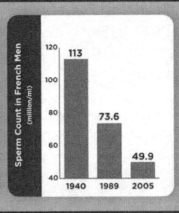

Source: Thoma, M., et al, "Prevalence of infertility in the United States as estimated by the current duration approach and a traditional construct approach," Fertility and Sterility, April 2013.
Slama, R., et al, "Estimation of the frequency of involuntary infertility on a nation-wide basis," Human Reproduction, 2012.
Karmaus, W., et al, "Infertility and subfecundity in population-based samples

Source: Dunson, D., et al, "Changes with age in the level and duration of fertility in the menstrual cycle," Human Reproduction, 2002. Coulam, C., et al, "Association between Major Histocompatibility Antigen and Reproductive Performance," American Journal of Reproductive Immunology and Microbiology, 1987. Ober, C., "Human leukocyte antigen matching and fetal loss: results of a 10 year prospective study, Human Reproduction, 1998.

The Death of the European Culture

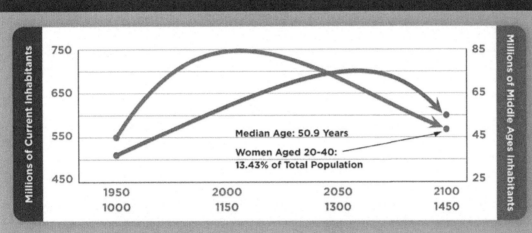

Source: United Nations Population Division - World Population Prospects: The 2017 Revision
Medieval Sourcebook (Fordham University)

The Path of St. Joseph

"When [Joseph] heard that Archelaus reigned over Judea in place of his father Herod, he was afraid to go there, and being warned in a dream he withdrew to the district of Galilee. And he went and dwelt in a city called Nazareth" (Matthew 2:22-23).

"Is it lawful to pay taxes to Caesar, or not?... Render therefore to Caesar the things that are Caesar's, and to God the things that are God's" (Matthew 22:17-21).

"Let us make man in our image, after our likeness" (Genesis 1:26).

- How is this culture "attacking your fatherhood?"

- How can you better inform yourself about the reality of our current culture? Would you be interested in a special course from Paradisus Dei?

- How can you help your children to clearly distinguish between the "things of Caesar and the things of God?"

Next Week

The 2nd Day:
Religious Turmoil

SESSION 17

The 2nd Day:
Religious Turmoil

Weekly Plan

1. Apply experience of Holy Family to today.
2. Consider the response of St. Joseph.
3. Paradisus Dei New Springtime Prayer
4. Divine Mercy Chaplet
5. Listen to the voice of the Holy Spirit.
6. List how our family is impacted.
7. List plan of action.

A Novena in Nazareth

1. The Roman Empire
2. Religious Turmoil
3. Social Context: Hardening of the Heart
4. The Annunciation
5. The Flight into Egypt
6. The Home at Nazareth
7. The Wedding Feast at Cana
8. The Passion
9. Pentecost

TMIY

Religious Life in the Time of the Holy Family

"A dissension arose between the Pharisees and the Sadducees; and the assembly was divided. For the Sadducees say that there is no resurrection, nor angel, nor spirit; but the Pharisees acknowledge them all... the dissension became violent" (Acts 23:7-10).

"Jews demand signs and Greeks seek wisdom" (1 Corinthians 1:22).

TMIY

Religious Confusion

> "Then I saw another beast which rose out of the earth; it had two horns like a lamb and it spoke like a dragon. It exercises all the authority of the first beast in its presence, and makes the earth and its inhabitants worship the first beast... it deceives those on earth" (Revelation 13:11—13:14).

> "The time of clear doctrine extended from Hadrian... It is certain that we are living in it; it is certain also that it will last until the downfall of the beast... and peace will be given. But first, tribulation must come to pass" (16.19).

Source: Bonaventure, Collationes in Heaxaemeron, The Works of Bonaventure, v. 5, St. Anthony Guide Press, Patterson, N.J., 1970, p. 241.

TMIY

The Mystery of Paradise

The Garden of Eden	Agony in the Garden	Resurrection in the Garden	The Eschatological Garden
"The LORD God planted a garden in Eden, in the east" (Genesis 2:8).	"There was a garden, which he and his disciples entered" (John 18:1).	"In the place where he was crucified there was a garden" (John 19:41).	"Then he showed me... the tree of life" (Revelation 22:1-2).

The Temple

The Church

The Holy Family

TMIY

Martin Luther

Tower Experience (~1518)	"At last, by the mercy of God... I began to understand that the righteousness of God is that by which the righteous lives by a gift of God, namely by faith ... Here I felt that I was altogether born again and had entered paradise itself through open gates."
Sola Fide	"So nothing is required of us but faith alone, whereby we apprehend Christ, and believe that our sins and our death are condemned and abolished in the sin and death of Christ."
Sola Scriptura	"Therefore all Christians should stand strong and steadfast upon the Word alone."

Source: Dillenberger, J., "Martin Luther – Selections from His Writings," Anchor Books, 1962, p. 11; p. 121; and p. 243.

TMIY

The Philosophy of Voltaire

> Be sure that a she-ass spoke; believe that a fish swallowed up a man and threw him on the shore three days later safe and sound; don't doubt that the God of the universe ordered... [a Jewish] prophet to buy two whores and to beget sons of them... Believe a hundred things either obviously abominable or mathematically impossible; otherwise the God of mercy will burn you in the fires of hell throughout all eternity...
>
> **Voltaire**
> Philosophical Dictionary

Source: Voltaire, "Philosophical Dictionary," Penguin Books, New York, NY, 1972, p. 58.

TMIY

The Rise of Secularization

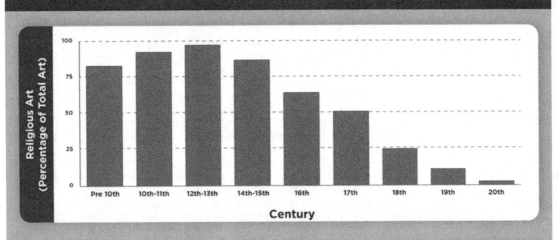

Source: Sorokin, P., "Cultural Dynamics," v. 1, American Book Company, 1937, p. 382.

TMIY

The Theory of Evolution

"In considering the origin of species, it is quite conceivable that a naturalist... might come to the conclusion that species had not been independently created, but had descended, like varieties from other species."

Super Fecundity	"More individuals of each species are born than can possibly survive."
Fitness	"There is a frequently recurring struggle for existence... if any being vary however slightly in any manner profitable to itself..."
Natural Selection	(i.e. Survival of the Fittest) "...it will have a better chance of surviving, and thus be naturally selected."
Evolution	"Based on the principle of inheritance, any selected variety will tend to propagate its new and modified form."

Source: Darwin, C., "The Origin of Species," Random House, New York, NY, 1993, pp. 19-21.

TMIY

The Growth in "Disbelief"

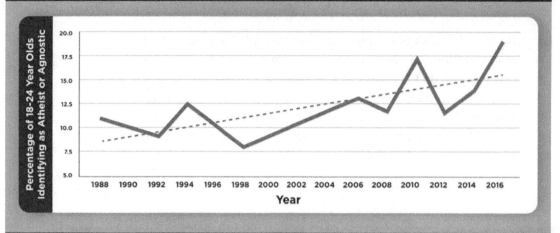

Source: General Social Survey 1972-2016.

TMIY

The Need for Wisdom

"Also it causes all... to be marked on the right hand or the forehead, so that no one can buy or sell unless he has the mark, that is, the name of the beast or the number of its name. This calls for wisdom: let him who has understanding reckon the number of the the beast, for it is a human number, its number is six hundred and sixty-six" (Revelation 13:16-18).

"Children, it is the last hour; and as you have heard that antichrist is coming, so now many antichrists have come... This is the antichrist, he who denies the Father and the Son" (1 John 2:18-22).

To express the superlative, ancient languages used repetition: "Holy, holy, holy, is the Lord God Almighty" (Revelation 4:8).

"The Antichrist's deception already begins to take shape in the world every time the claim is made to realize within history that messianic hope which can only be realized beyond history... The Church has rejected even modified forms of this falsification of the kingdom... Especially the 'intrinsically perverse' political form of secular messianism'" (Catechism #676).

TMIY

Jesus Christ and the Three Wisdoms

Natural Knowledge	"Look at the birds of the air: they neither sow nor reap nor gather into barns, and yet your heavenly Father feeds them. Are you not of more value than they?... your heavenly Father knows that you need them all. But seek first his kingdom and his righteousness, and all these things shall be yours as well" (Matthew 6:26-33).
Divine Revelation	"It is written, 'Man shall not live by bread alone, but by every word that proceeds from the mouth of God'" (Matthew 4:4).
"Contemplative" Knowledge	"That the dead are raised, even Moses showed, in the passage about the bush, where he calls the Lord the God of Abraham and the God of Isaac and the God of Jacob. Now he is not God of the dead, but of the living" (Luke 20:37-38).

TMIY

SESSION 17

- In what ways is your family being impacted by the secular culture in which we live?

- How is our scientific culture working to undermine your faith and that of your children?

- In what ways do you and/or your children believe that "technology will save us?"

Next Week

The 3rd Day:
Social Context: Hardening of the Heart

The 3rd Day:
Cultural Context:
The Hardening of the Heart

Weekly Plan

1. Apply experience of Holy Family to today.
2. Consider the response of St. Joseph.
3. Paradisus Dei New Springtime Prayer
4. Divine Mercy Chaplet
5. Listen to the voice of the Holy Spirit.
6. List how our family is impacted.
7. List plan of action.

A Novena in Nazareth

1. The Roman Empire
2. Religious Turmoil
3. Social Context: Hardening of the Heart
4. The Annunciation
5. The Flight into Egypt
6. The Home at Nazareth
7. The Wedding Feast at Cana
8. The Passion
9. Pentecost

TMIY

The Question of Justice and Mercy

The scribes and the Pharisees brought a woman who had been caught in adultery, and placing her in the midst they said to [Jesus], "Teacher, this woman has been caught in the act of adultery. Now in the law Moses commanded us to stone such. What do you say about her?"... Jesus bent down and wrote with his finger on the ground. And as they continued to ask him, he stood up and said to them, "Let him who is without sin among you be the first to throw a stone at her." And once more he bent down and wrote with his finger on the ground.

John 8:3-8

TMIY

The Hardening of the Heart

And Pharisees came up to [Jesus] and tested him by asking, "Is it lawful to divorce one's wife for any cause?" He answered, "Have you not read that he who made them from the beginning made them male and female, and said, 'For this reason a man shall leave his father and mother and be joined to his wife, and the two shall become one'? So they are no longer two but one. What therefore God has joined together, let no man put asunder." They said to him, "Why then did Moses command one to give a certificate of divorce, and to put her away?" He said to them, "For your hardness of heart Moses allowed you to divorce your wives..."

Matthew 19:3-8

TMIY

The Destruction of the Temple and Israel

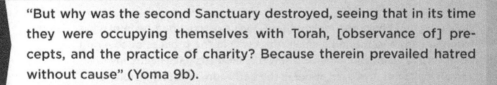

"But why was the second Sanctuary destroyed, seeing that in its time they were occupying themselves with Torah, [observance of] precepts, and the practice of charity? Because therein prevailed hatred without cause" (Yoma 9b).

"Jerusalem was destroyed... because they based their judgments [strictly] upon Biblical law, and did not go beyond the requirements of the law" (Baba Mezia, 30b).

Source: Babylonian Talmud, The Soncino Press, New York, 1986, Tractate Yoma 9b; Tractate Baba Mezia 30b.

TMIY

The Cosmic Week

It should be noted that as God created the world in six days and rested on the seventh, so also the mystical body of Christ has six ages... Hence, Scripture describes [the course of the world] in relation to the times of origin, of symbolism, and of grace or salvation... The times of symbols were seven in number: the times of the founding of nature, the cleansing of sin, the choosing of a people, the establishment of the law, the glory of the kings, the voice of the prophets, and the intermediate response.

Bonaventure
Collationes in Heaxaeme, 15.12, 16.11, 16.12

Source: Bonaventure, Collationes in Heaxaemeron, The Works of Bonaventure, v. 5, St. Anthony Guide Press, Patterson, N.J., 1970, p. 223; p. 236.

TMIY

The Seven Letters

Church	Ephesus	Smyrna	Pergamum	Thyatira	Sardis	Philadelphia	Laodicea
Issue	"You have abandoned the love you had at first" (Revelation 2:4).	"The devil is about to throw some of you into prison, that you may be tested" (Revelation 2:10).	"Some... hold the teaching of Balaam, who taught Balak to put a stumbling block before... Israel" (Revelation 2:14).	"You tolerate the woman Jezebel... beguiling my servants to practice immorality" (Revelation 2:20).	"You have the name of being alive, and you are dead... I have not found your works perfect"(Revelation	"I know that you have but little power" (Revelation 3:8).	"You are neither cold nor hot... because you are lukewarm... I will spew you out of my mouth" (Revelation 3:15-16).
History of Israel	Adam and Eve	Abraham	Exodus	Davidic Kingdom	Babylonian Captivity	Return to Israel	Time of Christ
	Committed Original Sin and then hid from God.	The Jews are led into the Egyptian captivity.	Israel's journey for 40 years in the desert where they encountered Balaam and Balak.	Idolatry in Israel and the splitting of the Kingdom in two.	Destruction of Israel and the leading into the Babylonian captivity.	A remnant returns to Israel to rebuild the Temple.	Apparent fervor, but "their heart is far from me" (Matthew 15:8).

Source: Corsini, E., "The Apocalypse: The Perennial Revelation of Jesus Christ," Michael Glazier, Inc., 1983, pp. 105-109.

> Only once did I have the feeling that [God] existed. I had been playing with matches and burned a small rug. I was in the process of covering up my crime when suddenly God saw me. I felt His gaze inside my head and on my hands. I whirled about in the bathroom, horribly visible, a live target. Indignation saved me. I flew into a rage against so crude an indiscretion, I blasphemed, I muttered like my grandfather: 'God damn it, God damn it, God damn it.' He never looked at me again."

Jean-Paul Sartre

Source: Sartre, "The Words – The Autobiography of Jean-Paul Sartre," Vintage Books, 1981, p. 102.

Jean-Paul Sartre and the End of Love

- Man is absolute freedom: Man is "condemned to be free... No limits to my freedom can be found except freedom itself or if you prefer, that we are not free to cease being free."

- Love is IMPOSSIBLE since it would entail the loss of freedom.

- "While I attempt to free myself from the hold of the other, the other is trying to free himself from mine; while I seek to enslave the other, the other seeks to enslave me... Conflict is the original meaning of being-for-others."

- "Hell is other people."

Source: "Being and Nothingness," translated by Barnes, H., Philosophical Library, 1956, p. 439 and p. 364. Sartre, "No Exit," (Play), May, 1944.

The "Curse" Laid Upon Woman

"The worst curse that was laid upon woman was that she should be excluded from those warlike forays. For it is not in giving life but in risking life that man is raised above the animal; that is why superiority has been accorded in humanity not to the sex that brings forth but to that which kills."

"No woman should be authorized to stay at home to raise her children. Women should not have that choice, precisely because if there is such a choice, too many women will make that one... as long as the family and the myth of the family and the myth of maternity and the maternal instinct are not destroyed, women will still be oppressed."

"One million women in France have an abortion every year... These women are veiled in silence. I declare that I am one of them. I have had an abortion. Just as we demand free access to birth control, we demand the freedom to have an abortion" (Manifesto of the 343, 1971).

Source: de Beauvoir, "The Second Sex," Everyman's Library, 1993, p. 64.
"Sex, Society, and the Female Dilemma – A Dialogue between Simone de Beauvoir and Betty Friedan," Saturday Review, June 14, 1975.
Moi, T., "Simone de Beauvoir: The Making of an Intellectual Woman," Oxford University Press, 2009.

TMIY

The Neurological Reality of Love

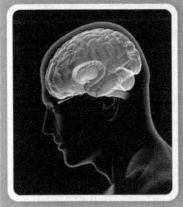

Oxytocin simultaneously activates brain circuitry for attachment (anterior cingulate, lateral septum, and middle insula) and trust (deactivation of the amygdala and dorsal striatum).

When the attachment is broken, our trust is broken.

Brain circuitry for social pain and physical pain overlap: the dorsal anterior cingulate cortex (dACC) and the right ventral prefrontal cortex (RVPFC).

A broken attachment physically hurts.

Feedback loop in reward circuitry: "Don't repeat a painful experience."

Source: Wang, Z., et al., "Neurochemical regulation of pair bonding in male prairie voles," Physiology and Behavior, 2004.
Acevedo, B., et al., "Neural correlates of long-term intense romantic love," Oxford Journals, Social Cognitive and Affective Neuroscience, 2011.
Naumgartner, T., et al., "Oxytocin Shapes the Neural Circuitry of Trust and Trust Adaptation in Humans," Neuron, v. 58, pp. 639-650, May 22, 2008.
Eisenberger, N., et al, "Why Rejection Hurts: A Common Neural Alarm System for Physical and Social Pain," Trends in Cognitive Science, July, 2008.

TMIY

The Hardening of the Heart

More than half of children under 18 do not live in a home with their biological mother and father.

Strained attachment between parent and child leads to later attachment issues.

Approximately 94 percent of Americans have sexual intercourse before marriage.

Most common timing of sex is BEFORE the relationship begins.

Hookups twice as likely as first dates on college campus.

Most students admit to wanting emotional intimacy, but are scared. Many – especially women – think that a hookup is the only way to enter into a relationship.

Since the vast majority of sexually active relationships will not lead to marriage, these relationships necessarily lead to pain – emotional and physical.

Sexually active 14-17 year olds are approximately 3 times more likely to be depressed and to attempt suicide.

Hardening of the heart as a protection measure.

Studies estimate that one-third of those in their early 20's will never marry.

Source: Pew Research Center, "Fewer than half of U.S. kids today live in a 'traditional family,'" December 22, 2014.
Komisar, E., "Being There: Why Prioritizing Motherhood in the First Three Years Matters," A TarcherPerigee Book, 2017, pp. 60-67.
Regnerus, M., "Cheap Sex: The Transformation of Men, Marriage and Monogamy," Oxford University Press, 2017, p. 99, 97, 165.
Garcia, J., et al., "Sexual Hookup Culture: A Review," Review of General Psychology, 2012, Vol. 16, No. 2, pp. 161-176.
Bradshaw, C., et al., "To Hook Up or Date: Which Gender Benefits?" Sex Roles, May 2010, Vol. 62, Issue 9-10, pp. 661-669.
Rector, R., "Sexually Active Teenagers are More Likely to be Depressed and to Attempt Suicide," The Heritage Foundations, 2003.
Eisenberger, N., et al., "Why Rejection Hurts: A Common Neural Alarm System for Physical and Social Pain," Trends in Cognitive Science, July, 2008.

TMIY

Mercy in St. Joseph's Heart

> Now the birth of Jesus Christ took place in this way. When his mother Mary had been betrothed to Joseph, before they came together she was found to be with child of the Holy Spirit; and her husband Joseph, being a just man and unwilling to put her to shame, resolved to send her away quietly. But as he considered this, behold, an angel of the Lord appeared to him in a dream, saying, "Joseph, son of David, do not fear to take Mary your wife, for that which is conceived in her is of the Holy Spirit..." When Joseph woke from sleep, he did as the angel of the Lord commanded him...
>
> Matthew 1:18-24

TMIY

TMIY
THAT MAN IS YOU!

SESSION 18

- How do you experience the "hardening of the heart" in your own life, and how is it impacting your children?

- How can you chose the path of mercy in all your daily actions as a means to keep a living heart?

- How can you help your children learn the depth and beauty of Scripture?

Next Week

**The 4th Day:
The Annunciation**

SESSION 19

The 4th Day:
The Annunciation

Weekly Plan

1. Apply experience of Holy Family to today.
2. Consider the response of St. Joseph.
3. Paradisus Dei New Springtime Prayer
4. Divine Mercy Chaplet
5. Listen to the voice of the Holy Spirit.
6. List how our family is impacted.
7. List plan of action.

A Novena in Nazareth

1. The Roman Empire
2. Religious Turmoil
3. Social Context: Hardening of the Heart
4. The Annunciation
5. The Flight into Egypt
6. The Home at Nazareth
7. The Wedding Feast at Cana
8. The Passion
9. Pentecost

TMIY

Joy and Trial for the Holy Family

"In the sixth month the angel Gabriel was sent from God to a city of Galilee named Nazareth, to a virgin betrothed to a man whose name was Joseph... And [the angel Gabriel] came to her and said, "Hail, full of grace, the Lord is with you... you will conceive in your womb and bear a son, and you shall call his name Jesus... The Holy Spirit will come upon you and the power of the Most High will overshadow you; therefore the child to be born will be called holy, the Son of God"" (Luke 1:26-35).

"Now the birth of Jesus Christ took place in this way. When his mother Mary had been betrothed to Joseph, before they came together she was found to be with child of the Holy Spirit; and her husband Joseph, being a just man and unwilling to put her to shame, resolved to send her away quietly" (Matthew 1:18-19).

"Behold, this child is set for the fall and rising of many in Israel, and for a sign that is spoken against (and a sword will pierce through your own soul also), that thoughts out of many hearts may be revealed" (Luke 2:34-35).

TMIY

The Reality of the Cross

> "Then I saw another mighty angel coming down from heaven... He had a little scroll open in his hand... Then the voice which I had heard from heaven spoke to me again, saying, "Go, take the scroll... Take it and eat; it will be bitter to your stomach, but sweet as honey in your mouth"" (Revelation 10:1-9).

> "[Jesus] said to all, "If any man would come after me, let him deny himself and take up his cross daily and follow me. For whoever would save his life will lose it; and whoever loses his life for my sake, he will save it"" (Luke 9:23-24).

TMIY

The Mystery of Paradise

The Garden of Eden	Agony in the Garden	Resurrection in the Garden	The Eschatological Garden
The Temple		**The Church**	
"The LORD God planted a garden in Eden, in the east" (Genesis 2:8).	"There was a garden, which he and his disciples entered" (John 18:1).	"In the place where he was crucified there was a garden" (John 19:41).	"Then he showed me... the tree of life" (Revelation 22:1-2).

The Holy Family

TMIY

The Teaching of Pope St. Paul VI

 The teaching [in *Humanae Vitae*]... is founded upon the inseparable connection, willed by God... Between the two meanings of the conjugal act: the unitive meaning and the procreative meaning... By safeguarding both these essential aspects, the unitive and procreative, the conjugal act preserves in its fullness the sense of true mutual love and its ordination towards man's most high calling to parenthood... To tell the truth, the Church is not surprised to be made, like her divine founder, a 'sign of contradiction.'

Pope St. Paul VI
Humanae Vitae, #12 and #17

TMIY

The "Prophecy" of Pope St. Paul VI

> Let them consider, first of all, how wide and easy a road would thus be opened up towards conjugal infidelity and the general lowering of morality... It is also to be feared that the man... may come to the point of considering her as a mere instrument of selfish enjoyment, and no longer as his respected and beloved companion. Let it be considered also that a dangerous weapon would thus be placed in the hands of those public authorities who take no heed of moral exigencies.
>
> **Pope St. Paul VI**
> *Humanae Vitae, #17*

TMIY

The Fulfillment of a Prophecy

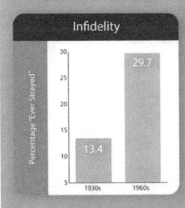

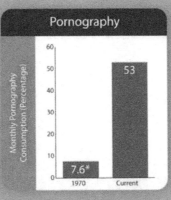

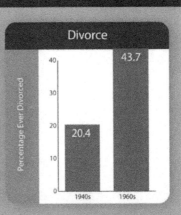

Source: General Social Survey, 1972-2010.
Source: 1970 Estimate based on Playboy circulation rate of 5.4 million
Source: General Social Survey

TMIY

The Prophet of a New Culture

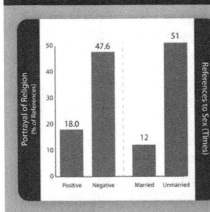

The media has become the primary means of education for faith and sexuality.

Formal religious institutions and clearly defined beliefs about God are presented negatively 2.5 times more frequently than positively.

Marriage is most frequently presented as burdensome and confining.

Spoken and visual references to unmarried sex outnumber those to married sex 4.25 to 1 in "Family Hour."

R-rated films contain an average of 8 acts of sexual intercourse.

Sources: Hjarvard, S., "The Mediatization of Religion,"
5th International Conference on Media, Religion, and Culture, Stockholm, 2006.
Parents Television Council, "Faith in a Box," December 2006.
Parents Television Council, "Happily Never After," August 5, 2008.
Strasburger, V., et al, "Children, Adolescents, and the Media," Third Edition, Sage Publications, 2014, p. 213.

TMIY

A Tool in the Hand of Governments

> Survey data suggest that approximately 120 million additional women world wide would be currently using a modern family-planning method if more accurate information and affordable services were easily available... These numbers do not include the substantial and growing numbers of sexually active unmarried individuals wanting and in need of information and services... To meet their needs and close the existing large gaps in services, family planning and contraceptive supplies will need to expand very rapidly over the next several years... All countries should take steps... by the year 2015... to provide universal access to a full range of safe and reliable family-planning methods.

International Conference on Population and Development
Cairo, Egypt, September 5-13, 1994
Plan of Action, Chapter 7

TMIY

A Sign of Contradiction

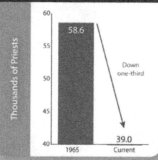

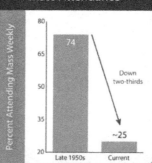

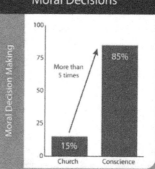

Source: "Frequently Requested Church Statistics," Center for Applied Research in the Apostolate (CARA), Georgetown University.

Source: The Gallup Poll, "Pray Tell: American's Stretching Truth about Church Attendance," University of Michigan, Institute for Social Research.

Source: USA Today/CNN/Gallup Poll (August 1993).

TMIY

Opening St. Joseph's Heart to Mercy

 "When his mother Mary had been betrothed to Joseph, *before they came together* she was found to be with child of the Holy Spirit" (Matthew 1:18).

 When Joseph woke from sleep, he did as the angel of the Lord commanded him; *he took his wife*" (Matthew 1:24).

 The trial of St. Joseph lies between these two great moments.

 The home at Nazareth is born of St. Joseph's trial. It is born when his heart is opened to his spouse in mercy.

TMIY

St. Joseph as the Image of Christ

"Husbands, love your wives, as Christ loved the church and gave himself up for her, that he might sanctify her... that he might present the church to himself in splendor, without spot or wrinkle or any such thing, that she might be holy and without blemish" (Ephesians 5:25-27).

"The messenger flies swiftly to the spouse, in order to remove every attachment to a human marriage from God's spouse. He does not take the Virgin away from Joseph but simply restores her to Christ... Christ, then, takes his own bride; he does not steal someone else's" (St. Peter Chrysologus).

TMIY

 The light of divine mercy... will illumine the way for the men and women of the third millennium... It is this love which must inspire humanity today... This consoling message is addressed above all to those who, afflicted by a particularly harsh trial... Have lost all confidence in life and are tempted to give in to despair. To them the gentle face of Christ is offered... How many souls have been consoled by the prayer, 'Jesus, I trust in you.'

Pope St. John Paul II
April 30, 2000

TMIY

 **SESSION 19**

THAT MAN IS YOU!

• **How can you open your heart and family to a greater practice of mercy?**

• **How can you better educate yourself and your children about the realities of our culture?**

• **What do you think of the "prophecy of Pope St. Paul VI" and the data showing its fulfillment?**

Next Week

The 5th Day:
The Flight into Egypt

SESSION 20

The 5th Day:
The Flight into Egypt

Weekly Plan

Apply experience of Holy Family to today. **1**

Consider the response of St. Joseph. **2**

Paradisus Dei New Springtime Prayer **3**

Divine Mercy Chaplet **4**

Listen to the voice of the Holy Spirit. **5**

List how our family is impacted. **6**

List plan of action. **7**

A Novena in Nazareth

1 The Roman Empire

2 Religious Turmoil

3 Social Context: Hardening of the Heart

4 The Annunciation

5 The Flight into Egypt

6 The Home at Nazareth

7 The Wedding Feast at Cana

8 The Passion

9 Pentecost

TMIY

The Flight into Egypt

> Behold, wise men from the East came to Jerusalem, saying, "Where is he who has been born king of the Jews?"... When Herod the king heard this, he was troubled, and all Jerusalem with him... Then Herod summoned the wise men secretly and ascertained from them what time the star appeared; and he sent them to Bethlehem... Now when [the Wise Men] had departed, behold, an angel of the Lord appeared to Joseph in a dream and said, "Rise, take the child and his mother, and flee to Egypt... for Herod is about to search for the child, to destroy him." And he rose and took the child and his mother by night, and departed to Egypt... Then Herod, when he saw that he had been tricked by the wise men, was in a furious rage, and he sent and killed all the male children in Bethlehem and in all that region who were two years old or under.
>
> **Matthew 2:1-16**

TMIY

The Mystery of Paradise

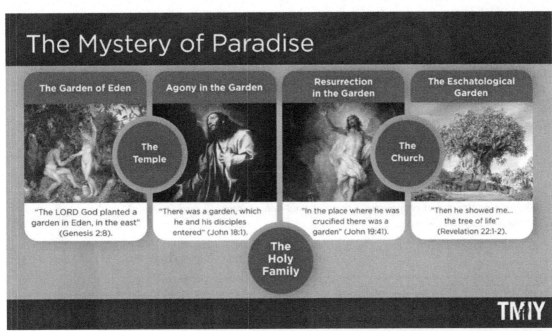

The Garden of Eden	Agony in the Garden	Resurrection in the Garden	The Eschatological Garden
"The LORD God planted a garden in Eden, in the east" (Genesis 2:8).	"There was a garden, which he and his disciples entered" (John 18:1).	"In the place where he was crucified there was a garden" (John 19:41).	"Then he showed me... the tree of life" (Revelation 22:1-2).

The Temple

The Church

The Holy Family

The Theology of the Garden

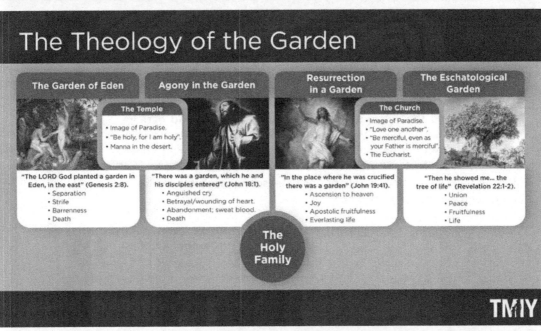

The Garden of Eden	Agony in the Garden	Resurrection in a Garden	The Eschatological Garden

The Temple
- Image of Paradise.
- "Be holy, for I am holy".
- Manna in the desert.

The Church
- Image of Paradise.
- "Love one another".
- "Be merciful, even as your Father is merciful".
- The Eucharist.

"The LORD God planted a garden in Eden, in the east" (Genesis 2:8).
- Separation
- Strife
- Barrenness
- Death

"There was a garden, which he and his disciples entered" (John 18:1).
- Anguished cry
- Betrayal/wounding of heart.
- Abandonment; sweat blood.
- Death

"In the place where he was crucified there was a garden" (John 19:41).
- Ascension to heaven
- Joy
- Apostolic fruitfulness
- Everlasting life

"Then he showed me... the tree of life" (Revelation 22:1-2).
- Union
- Peace
- Fruitfulness
- Life

The Holy Family

The Seven Seals

Seal	One	Two	Three	Four	Five	Six	Seven
Apocalypse	"I saw... a white horse, and its rider had a... crown... and he went out... conquering" (Revelation 6:2).	"Out came another horse, bright red; its rider was permitted to take peace from the earth" (Revelation 6:4).	"Behold, a black horse, and its rider had a balance... A quart of wheat... for a denarius"(Revelation 6:5-6).	"Behold, a pale horse, and its rider's name was Death, and Hades followed him" (Revelation 6:8).	"I saw under the altar... those who had been slain for the word of God" (Revelation 6:9).	"Behold, there was ...a great earthquake;... and the sun became black" (Revelation 6:12).	"There was silence in heaven for about half an hour" (Revelation 8:1).
	Christ Conquers	Strife	Bareness	Death	Tombs Opened	Earthquake	Holy Saturday
Jesus Christ	"This man performs many signs... every one will believe... in him" (John 11:47-48).	"Judas came... And with him a great crowd with swords and clubs" (Matthew 26:47).	"You will all fall away because of me this night... sweat became like.. great drops of blood" (Matthew 26:31; Luke 22:44).	"My soul is very sorrowful, even to death... into thy hands I commit my spirit" (Matthew 26:38; Luke 23:46).	"The tombs also were opened, and many bodies of the saints... were raised" (Matthew 27:52).	"The earth shook, and the rocks were split" (Matthew 27:51).	"Blessed indeed... that they may rest from their labors" (Revelation 14:13).

TMIY

A Vision of Don Bosco

I seemed to be strolling about a small plaza which opened into a vast plain where the Oratory boys were happily playing... They stopped playing and, looking very frightened, fled helter-skelter... Suddenly... I saw an enormous horse alight upon the ground. So huge was the animal that my blood ran cold... I kept thinking, 'What can this horse be?'... What a horror to see those ears and that frightful snout! At times it seemed to be carrying a load of riders; at other times it seemed to have wings. 'It must be a demon!' I exclaimed. Others were with me. 'What kind of monster is this?' I asked one of them. 'The red horse of the Apocalypse,' he replied.

St. John Bosco
July 5-6, 1862

Source: `Lemoyne, G., "The Biographical Memoirs of Saint John Bosco," Volume VII, Salesiana Publishers, New Rochelle, New York, 1972, pp. 128-129.

TMIY

The "Vision" of Pope St. John Paul II

Ricoeur has called Freud, Marx, and Nietzsche 'masters of suspicion', having in mind the whole system each one represents, and perhaps above all the hidden basis and the orientation of each in understanding and interpreting the humanum itself... the thinkers mentioned above, who have exercised and still exercise a great influence on the way of thinking and evaluating people of our time, seem in substance also to judge and accuse the human heart.

Pope St. John Paul II
October 29, 1980

TMIY

Ideologies of Evil and the Horsemen from Revelation

Hitler "Strife"	"Out came another horse, bright red; its rider was permitted to take peace from the earth" (Rev 6:4).
Communism "Barrenness"	"Behold, a black horse, and its rider had a balance... a quart of wheat for a denarius" (Revelation 6:5-6).
Sexual Revolution "Death"	"Behold, a pale horse, and its rider's name was Death, and Hades followed him" (Revelation 6:8).

Friedrich Nietzsche
Master of Suspicion
Karl Marx
Sigmund Freud

TMIY

Friedrich Nietzsche

 "I raise against the Christian church the most terrible of all accusations that any accuser ever uttered… I call Christianity the one great curse… I call it the one immortal blemish of mankind."

 "God is dead… we have killed him."

"Man is something that shall be overcome… All beings so far have created something beyond themselves… You have made your way from worm to man, and much in you is still worm… Behold, I teach you the overman."

"I felt for the first time that the strongest and highest Will to Life does not find expression in a miserable struggle for existence, but in a Will to War, a Will to Power, a Will to Overpower."

"I know my fate. One day there will be associated with my name the recollection of something frightful – of a crisis like no other before on earth… there will be wars such as there have never yet been on earth."

Source: "The Portable Nietzsche," Translated by Kaufmann, W., Penguin Books, 1954-1982, p. 655, p. 95, p. 124.
Forster-Nietzsche, "The Young Nietzsche," translated by Ludovici, A., London, 1912, p. 235.
Nietzsche, F., "Ecce Homo," Translated by Hollingdale, R., Penguin Classics, 2004,pp. 96-97.

TMIY

The Red Horse of the Apocalypse

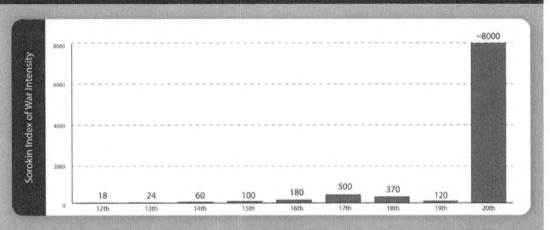

Source: Sorokin, P., "Social and Cultural Dynamics," v. 4, Table 49, p. 655. Author estimate for 20th Century extrapolated based upon Sorokin value after WWI.

TMIY

Karl Marx

 "Religion… is the sigh of the oppressed creature, the heart of a heartless world, and the soul of soulless conditions. It is the opium of the people. The abolition of religion as the illusory happiness of the people is the demand for their real happiness."

 "Individuals are dealt with only in so far as they are personifications of economic categories, embodiments of particular class-relations and class-interests."

 "The method of production in material life determines the general character of the social, political, and spiritual processes of life… It is not the consciousness of men that determines their being, but on the contrary, their social being determines their consciousness."

Source: "Contribution to the Critique of Hegel's Philosophy of Right," in "The Portable Karl Marx,"
Edited by Kamenka, E., Penguin Books, 1983, p. 115.
"Das Kapital," in "The Portable Karl Marx," Edited by Kamenka, E., Penguin Books, 1983, p. 435.
"The German Ideology," quoted in "Darwin, Marx, Wagner – Critique of a Heritage,"
Barzum, J., The University of Chicago Press, 1941-1981, p. 133.

TMIY

The Black Horse of the Apocalypse

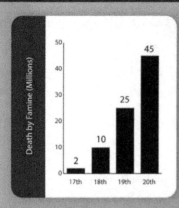

Death by Famine (Millions)

17th: 2
18th: 10
19th: 25
20th: 45

1917: "Peace, land, bread" – Vladimir Lenin.

1917: Communist Revolution followed by Civil War - 9 million deaths.

1921: 1 to 3 million die in Russian Famine.

1932-1934: 5 to 10 million die in Russian Famine.

1958-1961: 20-30 million die in Chinese Famine.

During the 1970's in Russia, food production increased 1% per year, one half of all farms operated at a loss, one-fifth to one-third of crops rotted in ground for lack of adequate storage, and food imports increased 1000%.

Source: Arnold, D., "Famine – Social Crisis and Historical Change," Basil Blackwell, 1991, p. 20.
Carroll, W., "The Rise and Fall of the Communist Revolution," Christendom Press, 1995, p. 695.

TMIY

Sigmund Freud and the Final Revolution

May 6, 1858 – September 23, 1939.

Cosmological revolution – Copernicus demonstrated that the earth was NOT the center of the universe.

Biological revolution – Darwin demonstrated that humanity was just the latest development in the evolution of animals.

Psychological revolution – Freud demonstrated that man is controlled by his unconscious and irrational drives.

"In Christian myth man's original sin is undoubtedly an offense against God the Father… [Christ] forces us to the conclusion that this sin was murder… He becomes a god himself beside or rather in place of his father. The religion of the son succeeds the religion of the father. As a sign of this substitution, the old totem feast is revived again in the form of communion in which the band of brothers now eats the flesh and blood of the son and no longer that of the father."

Source: "Totem and Taboo," Translated by Brill, A., Barnes and Noble Books, 1913 (2005), pp. 145.

TMIY

The Pale Horse of the Apocalypse

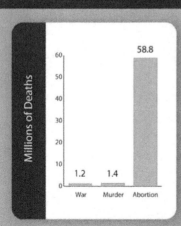

Millions of Deaths

War: 1.2
Murder: 1.4
Abortion: 58.8

Sigmund Freud is the recognized "father" of the sexual revolution.

The biological father has been removed from the home:
- 40% of children are born out-of-wedlock
- 54% of children live in a home without their biological father.

Removing the biological father from the home increases the likelihood of teenage sexual activity by 66.4%.

Forty-five percent of pregnancies are "unplanned." Forty percent are aborted.

Fifty-one percent of women were using contraception when they conceived child.

Almost 60 million babies have been aborted in the United States since the passage of Roe v. Wade in 1972.

Source: National Center for Health Statistics. Pew Research Center, "Fewer than half of U.S. kids today live in a 'traditional family,'" December 22, 2014. U.S. Department of Health and Human Services, "Teenagers in the United States: Sexual Activity, Contraceptive Use, and Childbearing,
2006-2010 National Survey of Family Growth," Vital and Health Statistics, Series 23, No. 31, October 2011, Table 2.
Guttmacher Institute, "Induced Abortion in the United States, January 2018. Guttmacher Institute, Centers for Disease Control.
U.S. Department of Veterans Affairs, America's Wars, Statistics, www.defense.gov/casualty.pdf.
Historical Statistics of the United States, Colonial Times to 1970, p. 414; Federal Bureau of Investigation, Universal Criminal Reporting Statistics, Number of Murders, 1960-Present; Author estimate for murders 1776-1899.

TMIY

The Fidelity of St. Joseph

"An angel of the Lord appeared to Joseph in a dream and said, "Rise, take the child and his mother, and flee to Egypt, and remain there till I tell you; for Herod is about to search for the child, to destroy him." And he rose and took the child and his mother by night, and departed to Egypt, and remained there until the death of Herod" (Matthew 2:13-15).

Joseph fled by night, which is by the darkness of faith.

We must embrace the teachings and guidance of Christ through his Church even in the darkness of faith.

TM1Y

SESSION 20

THAT MAN IS YOU!
BECOMING A MAN AFTER GOD'S OWN HEART

- How can you better understand the dramatic moments that we are currently passing through in the Church and Western society?

- How can you live a life of fidelity to Christ's direction like St. Joseph did when he fled into Egypt?

Next Week

**The 6th Day:
The Home at Nazareth**

SESSION 21

The 6th Day:
The Home at Nazareth

Weekly Plan

1. Apply experience of Holy Family to today.
2. Consider the response of St. Joseph.
3. Paradisus Dei New Springtime Prayer
4. Divine Mercy Chaplet
5. Listen to the voice of the Holy Spirit.
6. List how our family is impacted.
7. List plan of action.

A Novena in Nazareth

1. The Roman Empire
2. Religious Turmoil
3. Social Context: Hardening of the Heart
4. The Annunciation
5. The Flight into Egypt
6. The Home at Nazareth
7. The Wedding Feast at Cana
8. The Passion
9. Pentecost

TMIY

The Temple at Nazareth

"Now his parents went to Jerusalem every year at the feast of Passover. And when he was twelve years old... and when the feast was ended... the boy Jesus stayed behind in Jerusalem... supposing him to be in the company they went a day's journey... and when they did not find him, they returned to Jerusalem, seeking him. After three days they found him in the temple... and his mother said to him, 'Son, why have you treated us so? Behold, your father and I have been looking for you anxiously.' And he said to them... 'Did you not know that I must be in my Fathers house?'... And [Jesus] went down with them and came to Nazareth, and was obedient to them... And Jesus increased in wisdom and in stature, and in favor with God and man" (Luke 2:41-52).

"The secrets Mary had been in charge of revealing to Jesus, secrets wrapped in silence and darkness. Instead of opposing the one he called 'my Father' against the carpenter of Nazareth, Jesus, on the threshold of his conscious adolescence, had to see them both together in the same glance" (Fr. Andrew Doze).

Source: Doze, Fr. Andrew, "Saint Joseph: The Shadow of the Father," Trans. Audett, F., Alba House, New York, 1992, p. 67.

TMIY

The Holy Family: A Trinitarian Mystery

Jesus is the Word Incarnate	"And the Word became flesh and dwelt among us" (John 1:14).
Mary is overshadowed by the Holy Spirit	"The Holy Spirit will come upon you, and the power of the Most High will overshadow you" (Luke 1:35).
St. Joseph is the shadow of the Father	"Behold, your father and I have been looking for you anxiously" (Luke 2:48).

"It is therefore logical that Jesus is but of one heart with Mary; as a result, we can say that Mary is but of one heart with Joseph, and Joseph consequently is but of one heart with Jesus and Mary" (St. John Eudes, *Le Coeur Admirable, v. 8, Chapter 3*).

TMIY

The Seventh Trumpet

Then the seventh angel blew his trumpet, and there were loud voices in heaven, saying, "The kingdom of the world has become the kingdom of our Lord and of his Christ, and he shall reign for ever and ever..." Then God's temple in heaven was opened, and the ark of his covenant was seen within his temple.

Revelation 11:15-19

TMIY

The Mystery of Paradise

The Garden of Eden	Agony in the Garden	Resurrection in the Garden	The Eschatological Garden
"The LORD God planted a garden in Eden, in the east" (Genesis 2:8).	"There was a garden, which he and his disciples entered" (John 18:1).	"In the place where he was crucified there was a garden" (John 19:41).	"Then he showed me... the tree of life" (Revelation 22:1-2).

The Temple

The Church

The Holy Family

TMIY

"Man became the image of God not only through his own humanity, but also through the communion of persons, which man and woman form from the very beginning. The function of the image is that of mirroring the one who is the model, of reproducing its own prototype. Man becomes the image of God not so much in the moment of solitude as in the moment of communion."

Pope John Paul II
General Audience
November 14, 1979

The Creation of Humanity in Paradise

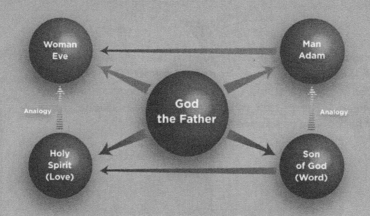

The Mystery of the Family in Redemption

In this great undertaking, which is the renewal of all things in Christ, marriage... becomes a new reality... We see that at the beginning of the New Testament, as at the beginning of the Old, there is a married couple. But whereas Adam and Eve were the source of evil which was unleashed on the world, Joseph and Mary are the summit from which holiness spreads over all the earth.

Pope St. John Paul II
Redemptoris Custos, #7

The Creation of Humanity in Paradise

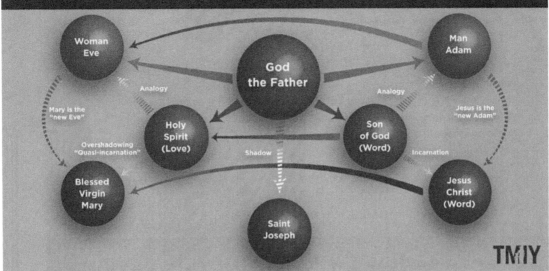

Marriage and the Mystery of Salvation

> **"** Can we not deduce that marriage has remained the platform for the realization of God's eternal plans, according to which the sacrament of creation had come near to human beings and prepared them for the sacrament of redemption, introducing them into the dimension of the work of salvation? The analysis of Ephesians, and in particular the 'classic' text of Ephesians 5:22-33, seems to lead toward such a conclusion.
>
> **Pope St. John Paul II**
> **General Audience**
> **October 13, 1982** **"**

> **"** The future of the world and of the Church pass by way of the family.
>
> **Pope St. John Paul II**
> *Familiaris Consortio, #75* **"**

The Kingdom of Heaven

> The kingdom of heaven is like a grain of mustard seed which a man took and sowed in his field; it is the smallest of all seeds, but when it has grown it is the greatest of shrubs and becomes a tree, so that the birds of the air come and make nests in its branches... The kingdom of heaven is like leaven which a woman took and hid in three measures of meal, till it was all leavened.
>
> *Matthew 13:31-33*

TMIY

The Importance of the Family

"Tell all the congregation of Israel that on the tenth day of this month they shall take every man a lamb according to their fathers' houses, a lamb for a household... This day shall be for you a memorial day, and you shall keep it as a feast to the LORD; throughout your generations... when your children say to you, 'What do you mean by this service?' you shall say, 'It is the sacrifice of the LORD'S passover, for he passed over the houses of the people of Israel in Egypt, when he slew the Egyptians'" (Exodus 12:3-27).

"And day by day, attending the temple together and breaking bread in their homes... praising God and having favor with all the people. And the Lord added to their number day by day those who were being saved" (Acts 2:46-47).

TMIY

St. Joseph and the Life of Prayer

"The same aura of silence that envelops everything else about Joseph also shrouds his work as a carpenter in the house of Nazareth. It is, however, a silence that reveals in a special way the inner portrait of the man. The Gospels speak exclusively of what Joseph 'did.' Still, they allow us to discover in his 'actions'... an aura of deep contemplation... The total sacrifice, whereby Joseph surrendered his whole existence to the demands of the Messiah's coming into his home, becomes understandable only in the light of his profound interior life" (St. John Paul II, *Redemptoris Custos, #25-26*).

"[Jesus] said to them... 'My house shall be called a house of prayer'" (Matthew 21:13).

TMIY

- How can you transform your home into "a house of prayer"?

- How can you teach your children how to enter more deeply into a devout prayer life?

- How can you better learn and defend the dignity of the family?

Next Week

**The 7th Day:
The Wedding Feast at Cana**

The 7th Day:
The Wedding Feast at Cana

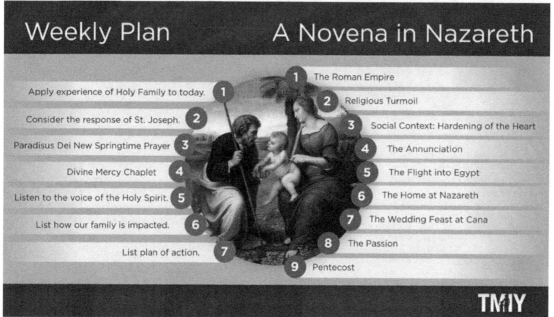

Weekly Plan

Apply experience of Holy Family to today. **1**

Consider the response of St. Joseph. **2**

Paradisus Dei New Springtime Prayer **3**

Divine Mercy Chaplet **4**

Listen to the voice of the Holy Spirit. **5**

List how our family is impacted. **6**

List plan of action. **7**

A Novena in Nazareth

1 The Roman Empire

2 Religious Turmoil

3 Social Context: Hardening of the Heart

4 The Annunciation

5 The Flight into Egypt

6 The Home at Nazareth

7 The Wedding Feast at Cana

8 The Passion

9 Pentecost

The Mystery of Paradise

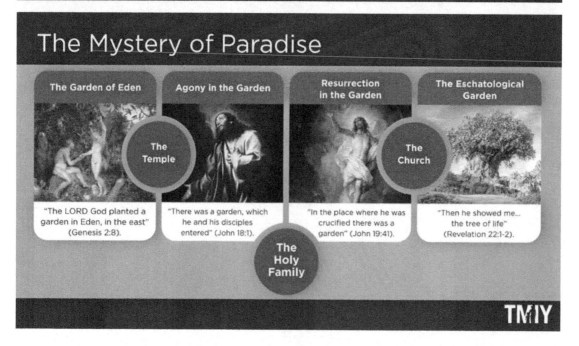

The Garden of Eden	Agony in the Garden	Resurrection in the Garden	The Eschatological Garden
"The LORD God planted a garden in Eden, in the east" (Genesis 2:8).	"There was a garden, which he and his disciples entered" (John 18:1).	"In the place where he was crucified there was a garden" (John 19:41).	"Then he showed me... the tree of life" (Revelation 22:1-2).

The Temple

The Church

The Holy Family

Water Flowing from Paradise

"A river flowed out of Eden to water the garden, and there it divided and became four rivers" (Genesis 2:10).

"Then he brought me back to the door of the temple; and behold, water was issuing from below the threshold of the temple toward the east... I saw upon the bank of the river very many trees on the one side and on the other... when [the river] enters the stagnant waters of the sea, the water will become fresh. And wherever the river goes every living creature which swarms will live... And on the banks, on both sides of the river, there will grow all kinds of trees for food. Their leaves will not wither nor their fruit fail, but they will bear fresh fruit every month, because the water for them flows from the sanctuary. Their fruit will be for food, and their leaves for healing" (Ezekiel 47:1-12).

TMIY

The Wedding Feast at Cana

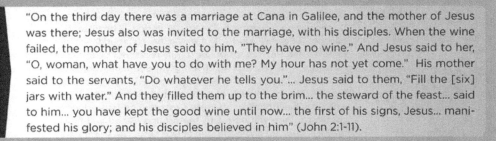

"On the third day there was a marriage at Cana in Galilee, and the mother of Jesus was there; Jesus also was invited to the marriage, with his disciples. When the wine failed, the mother of Jesus said to him, "They have no wine." And Jesus said to her, "O, woman, what have you to do with me? My hour has not yet come." His mother said to the servants, "Do whatever he tells you."... Jesus said to them, "Fill the [six] jars with water." And they filled them up to the brim... the steward of the feast... said to him... you have kept the good wine until now... the first of his signs, Jesus... manifested his glory; and his disciples believed in him" (John 2:1-11).

"Behold, the days are coming... [when] the mountains shall drip sweet wine, and all the hills shall flow with it" (Amos 9:13).

TMIY

A Great Sign in Heaven

And a great portent appeared in heaven, a woman clothed with the sun, with the moon under her feet, and on her head a crown of twelve stars; she was with child and she cried out in her pangs of birth, in anguish for delivery. And another portent appeared in heaven; behold, a great red dragon, with seven heads and ten horns, and seven diadems upon his heads... And the dragon stood before the woman who was about to bear a child... but her child was caught up to God... Now war arose in heaven, Michael and his angels fighting against the dragon... And the great dragon was thrown down... to the earth... woe to you, O earth and sea, for the devil has come down to you in great wrath, because he knows that his time is short!

Revelation 12:1-12

TMIY

The Vision of Our Lady

'A great sign,' thus the Apostle St. John describes a vision divinely sent him, appears in the heavens: 'A woman clothed with the sun, and with the moon under her feet and a crown of twelve stars upon her head' (Apocalypse 12:1). John therefore saw the Most Holy Mother of God already in eternal happiness, yet travailing in a mysterious childbirth. What birth was it? Surely it was the birth of us who, still in exile, are yet to be generated to the perfect charity of God, and to eternal happiness. And the birth pains show the love and desire with which the Virgin from heaven above watches over us, and strives with unwearying prayer to bring about the fulfillment of the number of the elect.

Pope St. Pius X
Ad diem illum laetissiumum, #24

TMIY

The Miraculous Medal Apparition

The times are very evil. Sorrows will come upon France; the throne will be overturned. The whole world will be upset by miseries of every kind... There will be an abundance of sorrows; and the danger will be great. Yet do not be afraid... I shall be with you myself... I will grant you many graces... The moment will come when the danger will be enormous; it will seem that all will be lost; at that moment, I will be with you; have confidence... the Cross will be treated with contempt; they will hurl it to the ground. Blood will flow; they will open up again the side of Our Lord. The streets will stream with blood... the whole world will be in sadness.

Our Lady to St. Catherine Laboure
July 18, 1830

Source: Dirvin, J., "Saint Catherine Laboure of the Miraculous Medal," Tan Books and Publishers, 1984.

TMIY

The Miraculous Medal Apparition

"Come to the foot of the altar. There graces will be shed upon all, great and little, who ask for them" (July 18, 1830).

"[Mary's] arms swept wide in a gesture of motherly compassion, while from her jeweled fingers the rays of light streamed upon the white globe at her feet. An oval formed around the Blessed Virgin: 'O Mary, conceived without sin, pray for us who have recourse to thee.' Have a medal struck after this model. All who wear it will receive great graces. They should wear it around the neck. Graces will abound for persons who wear it with confidence" (November 27, 1830).

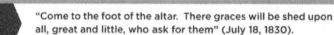

Source: Dirvin, J., "Saint Catherine Laboure of the Miraculous Medal," Tan Books and Publishers, 1984.

TMIY

The Apparition of Our Lady at Lourdes

Our Lady makes 18 apparitions to Bernadette Soubirous between February 11-July 16, 1858.

Feb 18th	"I do not promise to make you happy in this world but in the other."
Feb 24th	Feb 24th - Penance, penance, penance! Pray to God for the conversion of sinners. Go and kiss the ground as a penance for sinners."
Feb 25th	Feb 25th - the Spring of Lourdes is revealed: "Go and drink at the spring and wash yourself in it."
Mar 2nd	Mar 2nd - "Go and tell the priests that people are to come here in procession and to build a chapel here."
Mar 25th	Mar 25th - "I am the Immaculate Conception."

Source: Laurentin, R., "Bernadette of Lourdes," Darton, Longman and Todd, Ltd., 1999.
Sanctuary of Our Lady of Lourdes website: www.en.lourdes-france.org

TMIY

Grace Flowing through the Family

"Behold, water was issuing from below the threshold of the temple" (Ezekiel 47:1).

St. Catherine Laboure: "It's the same one!"

St. Catherine Laboure takes Our Lady for her mother. St. Bernadette takes St. Joseph for her father.

The Holy Family is hidden at Lourdes.

"Mary makes Bernadette enter into the particularly special atmosphere of the family... Mary makes the Chrsitians take the road to the Holy Family, where the Gospel is lived in its plentitude" (Fr. Andrew Doze).

A river of grace for the healing of the nations is flowing from

Source: Laurentin, R., "Bernadette of Lourdes," Darton, Longman and Todd, Ltd., 1999.
Laurentine, R., "Catherine Laboure: Visionary of the Miraculous Medal," Pauline Books and Media, 2006.
Doze, Fr. Andrew, "Saint Joseph: The Shadow of the Father," Trans. Audett, F., Alba House, 1992.

TMIY

The Apparition of Our Lady at Fatima

Our Lady appears to three peasant children six times between May 13 - October 13, 1917.

"You have seen hell where the souls of poor sinners go. To save them, God wishes to establish in the world devotion to my Immaculate Heart... When you see a night illumined by an unknown light, know that this is the great sign given you by God that He is about to punish the world for its crimes, by means of war, famine, and persecutions of the Church and of the Holy Father... Russia will spread her errors throughout the world, causing wars and persecutions of the Church. The good will be martyred; the Holy Father will have much to suffer; various nations will be annihilated."

Source: "Fatima in Lucia's own Words," edited by Fr. Louis Kondor, SVD, The Ravengate Press, 1989, pp. 104-105.

TMIY

The Vision of the Holy Family

Our Lady appears to three peasant children six times between May 13 – October 13, 1917.

"'Continue always to pray the Rosary every day'... Then, opening her hands, she made them reflect on the sun, and as she ascended, the reflection of her own light continued to be projected on the sun itself... After Our Lady had disappeared into the immense distance of the firmament, we beheld St. Joseph with the Child Jesus and Our Lady robed in white with a blue mantle, beside the sun. St. Joseph and the Child Jesus appeared to bless the world, for they traced the Sign of the Cross with their hands" (October 13, 1917).

Source: "Fatima in Lucia's own Words," edited by Fr. Louis Kondor, SVD, The Ravengate Press, 1989, pp. 169-170 and 104.

TMIY

The Spiritual Significance of Our Days

 The salvation of the world began through Mary and through her it must be accomplished. Mary scarcely appeared in the first coming of Jesus Christ... But in the second coming of Jesus Christ, Mary must be known and openly revealed by the Holy Spirit... God wishes therefore to reveal Mary, his masterpiece, and make her more known in these latter times... As she was the way by which Jesus first came to us, she will again be the way by which he will come to us the second time though not in the same manner.

St. Louis de Montfort
True Devotion to Mary

Source: St. Louis de Montfort, "True Devotion to Mary," 49—50, quoted in "God Alone: The Collected Writings of St. Louis Marie de Montfort," Montfort Publications, Bay Shore, NY, 1987, p. 303.

TMIY

St. Joseph and the Life of Prayer

 "Behold, I will send you Elijah the prophet before the great and terrible day of the LORD comes. And he will turn the hearts of fathers to their children and the hearts of children to their fathers, lest I come and smite the lands with a curse" (Malachi 4:5-6).

 St. Joseph's heart was always turned toward Jesus.

 At the last apparition of Fatima, St. Joseph appeared holding the Christ child.

TMIY

- How can you increase your devotion to St. Joseph?

- How can you allow St. Joseph to turn your heart towards your children?

- How well do you know the APPROVED apparitions of Our Lady? How can you become better informed?

Next Week

**The 8th Day:
The Passion**

SESSION 23

The 8th Day:
The Passion

Weekly Plan

1. Apply experience of Holy Family to today.
2. Consider the response of St. Joseph.
3. Paradisus Dei New Springtime Prayer
4. Divine Mercy Chaplet
5. Listen to the voice of the Holy Spirit.
6. List how our family is impacted.
7. List plan of action.

A Novena in Nazareth

1. The Roman Empire
2. Religious Turmoil
3. Social Context: Hardening of the Heart
4. The Annunciation
5. The Flight into Egypt
6. The Home at Nazareth
7. The Wedding Feast at Cana
8. The Passion
9. Pentecost

TMIY

The Mystery of Paradise

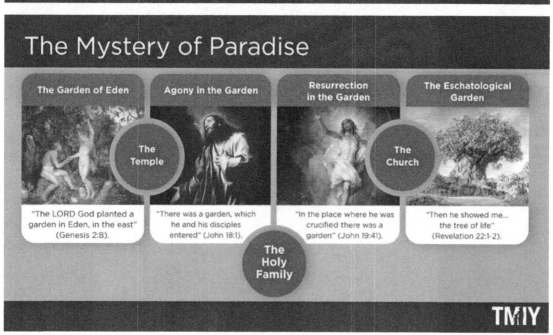

The Garden of Eden	Agony in the Garden	Resurrection in the Garden	The Eschatological Garden
The Temple		The Church	
"The LORD God planted a garden in Eden, in the east" (Genesis 2:8).	"There was a garden, which he and his disciples entered" (John 18:1).	"In the place where he was crucified there was a garden" (John 19:41).	"Then he showed me... the tree of life" (Revelation 22:1-2).

The Holy Family

TMIY

23-1

The Preparation: Transfiguration

> Jesus took with him Peter and James and John is brother, and led them up a high mountain apart. And he was transfigured before them, and his face shone like the sun, and his garments became white as light. And behold, there appeared to them Moses and Elijah, talking with him. And Peter said to Jesus, "Lord, it is well that we are here; if you wish, I will make three booths here, one for you and one for Moses and one for Elijah." He was still speaking, when lo, a bright cloud overshadowed them, and a voice from the cloud said, "This is my beloved Son, with whom I am well pleased; listen to him."
>
> **Matthew 17:1-5**

The Two Witnesses

> I will grant my two witnesses power to prophesy for one thousand two hundred and sixty days, clothed in sackcloth. These are the two olive trees and the two lampstands which stand before the Lord of the earth... They have power to shut the sky, that no rain may fall during the days of their prophesying, and they have power over the waters to turn them into blood, and to smite the earth with every plague, as often as they desire. And when they have finished their testimony, the beast that ascends from the bottomless pit will make war upon them and conquer them and kill them...
>
> **Revelation 11:3-7**

Our Lady and Elijah

"As [Elijah and Elisha] went on and talked, behold, a chariot of fire and horses of fire separated the two of them. And Elijah went up by a whirlwind into heaven" (2 Kings 2:11).

"The ever Virgin Mary, having completed the course of her earthly life, was assumed body and soul into heavenly glory" (Pope Pius XII, Munificentissimus Deus, #44).

"Yes, of course Mary's body was holy… Like the bodies of the saints, however, she has been held in honor for her character and understanding. And if I should say anything more in her praise, [she is] like Elijah, who was virgin from his mother's womb, always remained so, and was taken up and has not seen death" (St. Epiphanius).

Source: St. Epiphanius of Salamis, "Panarion,"Book III, Section 79, "The Panarion of Epiphanius of Salamis, Books II and III," Trans. Williams, F., Second Revised Edition, Leiden, Boston, MA, 2013, p. 641.

Our Lady in the Latter Times

 In the second coming of Jesus Christ, Mary must be known and openly revealed by the Holy Spirit so that Jesus may be know, loved and served through her... God wishes therefore to reveal Mary, his masterpiece, and make her more known in these latter times... Mary then must be better known than ever for the deeper understanding and the greater glory of the Blessed Trinity... God in these times wishes his Blessed Mother to be more known, loved and honored than she has ever been.

St. Louis de Montfort
True Devotion to Mary

Source: St. Louis de Montfort, "True Devotion to Mary," 49—55, quoted in "God Alone: The Collected Writings of St. Louis Marie de Montfort," Montfort Publications, Bay Shore, NY, 1987, pp. 303-305.

TMIY

Mary and the Passion of Christ

 "When the apostles fled, she stood before the Cross and gazed tenderly on the wounds of her Son, because she was waiting, not for her Son's death, but for the salvation of the world" (St. Ambrose).

 "At the time of the Passion... all the disciples of Christ with the exception of his mother had lost the faith, including St. John and Mary Magdalene (this at least is what the Fourth Gospel suggests), at this moment the Mother of Jesus, who was experiencing so much suffering in giving birth to the new people of God, turned out to be at the same time, in the strict sense, the sole representative of the Church" (Fr. Andre Feuillet).

Sources: Ambrose, "Expsitio, in Lucam 10, 132; SC 52, 200, quoted in Gambero, L., "Mary and the Fathers of the Church," Ignatius Press, San Francisco, 1999, p. 203. Feuilleet, A., "Jesus and His Mother – According to the Lucan Infancy Narratives, and the According to St. John," St. Bede's Publications, Still River, MA, 1974, p.

TMIY

The True Bread from Heaven

 "Then the LORD said to Moses, "Behold, I will rain bread from heaven for you; and the people shall go out and gather a day's portion every day"" (Exodus 16:4).

 "They said to [Jesus], "Then what sign do you do, that we may see, and believe you?... Our fathers ate the manna in the wilderness... Jesus then said to them, "Truly, truly, I say to you, it was not Moses who gave you the bread from heaven; my Father gives you the true bread from heaven. For the bread of God is that which comes down from heaven, and gives life to the world... I am the bread of life... For my flesh is food indeed, and my blood is drink indeed. He who eats my flesh and drinks my blood abides in me, and I in him" (John 6:30-56).

TMIY

St. John at the Foot of the Cross

"But standing by the cross of Jesus were his mother, and his mother's sister, Mary the wife of Clopas, and Mary Magdalene... when they came to Jesus and saw that he was already dead, they did not break his legs. But one of the soldiers pierced his side with a spear, and at once there came out blood and water. He who saw it has borne witness" (John 19:25-35).

"There flowed from his side blood and water. Beloved, do not pass over this mystery without thought; it has yet another hidden meaning, which I will explain to you. I said that the water and blood symbolized baptism and the holy Eucharist. From these two sacraments the Church is born" (St. John Chrysostom, Office of Readings, Good Friday).

TMIY

The Vision of the Two Columns

 This stately vessel is shielded by a flotilla escort. Winds and waves are with the enemy. In the midst of this endless sea, two solid columns... soar high into the sky: one is surmounted by a statue of the Immaculate Virgin... The other, far loftier and sturdier, supports a Host... The entire enemy fleet closes in to intercept and sink the flagship... They bombard it with everything they have... At times a formidable ram splinters a gaping hole into its hull... Suddenly, the Pope falls, seriously wounded... He is instantly helped up but, struck down a second time, dies... Breaking through all resistance, the new pope steers the ship safely between the two columns... The enemy ships panic and disperse.

Don Bosco

Source: Brown, E., et all, "Dreams, Visions and Prophecies of Don Bosco," Don Bosco Publications, New Rochelle, NY, 1986, pp. 105-108.

TMIY

Pope St. John Paul II and the Two Columns

 "The implementation of this programme of a renewed impetus in Christian living passes through the Eucharist... Let us take our place... At the school of the saints, who are the great interpreters of true Eucharistic piety" (Pope St. John Paul II, *Ecclesia de Eucharistia, #60-62*).

"A number of historical circumstances also make a revival of the Rosary quite timely... The family, the primary cell of society, [is] increasingly menaced by forces of disintegration on both the ideological and practical planes, so as to make us fear for the future of this fundamental and indispensible institution and, with it, for the future of society as a whole. The revival of the Rosary in Christian families... will be an effective aid to countering the devastating effects of this crisis typical of our age" (Pope St. John Paul II, *Rosarium Virginis Mariae, #6*).

TMIY

Developing Devotion to Christ and Our Lady

Devotion to Christ in the Eucharist

- Attend Mass as frequently as possible – including with your spouse and children.

- Daily Mass is particularly effective at focusing our attention on the Eucharist.

- Have a time of silence immediately after receiving the Eucharist and after Mass to speak with Jesus who is dwelling in your heart.

- Celebrate the major Feast Days in the liturgical calendar.

- Take time for Eucharistic Adoration.

Devotion to Our Lady

- Ask Christ for the grace to love his mother as he loves his mother.

- Wear the Miraculous Medal around your neck.

- Say five decades of the Rosary every day - over time you will recognize the power of the Rosary.

- Celebrate the Feast Days of Our Lady in the liturgical calendar.

- Read about APPROVED Marian apparitions.

TMIY

Entry into the Home at Nazareth

1	Enter into the home at Nazareth.
2	Offer our lists to Our Lady.
3	Pray the Rosary together.
4	Listen for the voice of Our Lady.
5	Drink of Lourdes water.
6	Pray Paradisus Dei's prayer for the New Springtime.
7	Do whatever God tells you.

TMIY

SESSION 23

THAT MAN IS YOU!

- What is the most spiritually significant moment you have had while receiving the Eucharist?

- How can you increase your devotion to the Eucharist?

- When have you most perceived Our Lady's presence?

- How can you increase your devotion to Our Lady?

Next Week

**The 9th Day:
The Pentecost**

SESSION 24

The 9th Day:
The Pentecost

Weekly Plan

Apply experience of Holy Family to today.	1
Consider the response of St. Joseph.	2
Paradisus Dei New Springtime Prayer	3
Divine Mercy Chaplet	4
Listen to the voice of the Holy Spirit.	5
List how our family is impacted.	6
List plan of action.	7

A Novena in Nazareth

1	The Roman Empire
2	Religious Turmoil
3	Social Context: Hardening of the Heart
4	The Annunciation
5	The Flight into Egypt
6	The Home at Nazareth
7	The Wedding Feast at Cana
8	The Passion
9	Pentecost

TMIY

The Mystery of Paradise

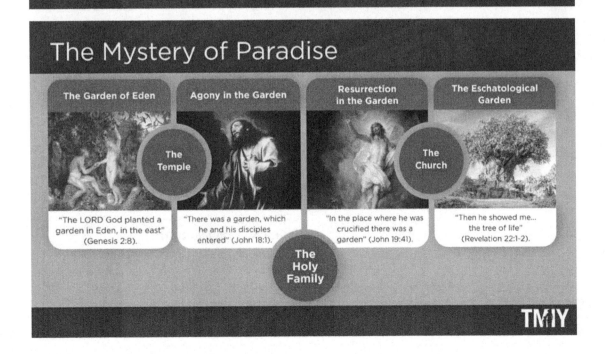

The Garden of Eden	Agony in the Garden	Resurrection in the Garden	The Eschatological Garden
"The LORD God planted a garden in Eden, in the east" (Genesis 2:8).	"There was a garden, which he and his disciples entered" (John 18:1).	"In the place where he was crucified there was a garden" (John 19:41).	"Then he showed me... the tree of life" (Revelation 22:1-2).

The Temple

The Church

The Holy Family

TMIY

The Gift of the Holy Spirit at Pentecost

All these with one accord devoted themselves to prayer together, with the women and Mary the mother of Jesus, and with his brethren... When the day of Pentecost had come, they were all together in one place. And suddenly a sound came from heaven like the rush of a mighty wind, and it filled all the house where they were sitting. And there appeared to them tongues as of fire, distributed and resting on each one of them. And they were all filled with the Holy Spirit and began to speak in other tongues, as the Spirit gave them utterance.

Acts 1:14; 2:1-4

A "New Pentecost"

"Renew in our own days your miracles as of a second Pentecost" (Pope St. John XXIII, Preparatory Prayer for Vatican II).

"Christ whom we have contemplated and loved bids us to set out once more on our journey... and urges us to share the enthusiasm of the very first Christians: we can count on the power of the same Spirit who was poured out at Pentecost and who impels us still today to start out anew, sustained by the hope 'which does not disappoint'" (Pope St. John Paul II, *Novo Millennio Ineunte, #58*).

The Apostles of the New Springtime

They will be true apostles of the latter times... They will have the two-edged sword of the Word of God in their mouths and the blood-stained standards of the Cross on their shoulders. They will carry the crucifix in their right hand and the rosary in their left, and the holy names of Jesus and Mary on their heart... Such are the great men who are to come.

St. Louis de Montfort
True Devotion to Mary

Source: St. Louis de Montfort, "True Devotion to Mary," 58—59, quoted in "God Alone: The Collected Writings of St. Louis Marie de Montfort," Montfort Publications, Bay Shore, NY, 1987, pp. 306-307.

The Defeat of Satan

> I saw an angel coming down from heaven, holding in his hand the key of the bottomless pit and a great chain. And he seized the dragon, that ancient serpent, who is the Devil and Satan, and bound him for a thousand years, and threw him into the pit, and shut it and sealed it over him, that he should deceive the nations no more, till the thousand years were ended. After that he must be loosed for a little while.
>
> *Revelation 20:1-3*

TMIY

The Sacred Heart Devotion

- "Behold the Heart which has so loved men that it has spared nothing, even to exhausting and consuming Itself, in order to testify It's love" (Words of Christ to St. Margaret Mary Alacoque, June 16, 1675).

- "I promise you in the excessive mercy of My Heart that Its all-powerful love will grant to all those who receive Holy Communion on nine first Fridays of the month consecutively, the grace of final repentance" (Words of Christ to St. Margaret Mary Alacoque, May, 1688).

- Good friend had a family member who had turned away from the faith and had become antagonistic towards Catholicism, the Pope, etc.

- Person wasn't practicing anything and had become quite disillusioned and bitter with life and was fairly alienated from the family.

- Not knowing what to do, my friend began to do the First Friday devotion for his family member.

- Before the end of the devotion, family member was reconciled to the Church and had a much more optimistic outlook on life and better relations with the entire family.

TMIY

Devotion to Our Lady

- Story from my own personal life.
- My father was in very ill health – the effects of being a very heavy smoker for 65 years.
- He wanted to stay in the house by himself – to die at home – although he couldn't take care of himself.
- Constant source of difficulties and tension with family members.
- Went into the hospital with COPD (Chronic Obstructive Pulmonary Disease).
- Saved him and sent him to rehab.
- I visited him and had never seen him worse. He could hardly move. Nonetheless, he wanted out of rehab to go back home.
- Asked me if I could help him find the Cross he wore around his neck. It had gotten lost at the hospital. No chance of finding it.
- I took the Miraculous Medal from my neck and placed it on his.
- When I arrived home, I told Shelly that I wasn't sure if I would ever see him alive again.
- Two days later, he was perfectly good and wanted to move into an assisted living home.

TMIY

Amici di Giuseppe – Friends of Joseph

1	Live the 7 Steps of Paradisus Dei/TMIY according to the heart of St. Joseph.	• "I have called you friends" (John 15:15). • Entry into a deeper, contemplative spirituality based on the model of St. Joseph where science gives way to the science of love. • Daily Rosary: "To contemplate the face of Christ and contemplate it with Mary." • Monthly/weekly messages at the "school of Mary and Joseph."
2	Gather together with other Amici di Giuseppe men at least once/month for prayer and discussion.	• "Small combat group" meets at least monthly. • Prayer: Mass and/or Rosary. • Discussion/support in living the 7 Steps.
3	Enroll through the TMIY app or online.	• Possibility of connecting with other Amici di Giuseppe members.
4	Sign of membership.	• A specifically designed Amici di Giuseppe Rosary.

TMIY

Missionaries to the Family

Spiritual Formation	Intellectual Formation	Practical Formation	Products for Apostolate
• Provide Missionaries a strong spiritual life based on marriage and family life. • Provided by Paradisus Dei. • Based upon the Holy Family as given in the 7 Steps.	• Provide Missionaries strong theological training. • Provided by 4 university professors. • Based upon the Four Pillars of the Catechism.	• Provide Missionaries the practical skills and knowledge necessary to work with families. • Provided by Paradisus Dei. • Focus: Working with parishes and working with individuals.	• Provide Missionaries the tools they need to engage and accompany families. • Provided by Paradisus Dei. • Based on lifecycle of the family. Four major products.

Formation Program Goals

TMIY

Entry into the Home at Nazareth

1. Enter into the home at Nazareth.
2. Offer our lists to Our Lady.
3. Pray the Rosary together.
4. Listen for the voice of Our Lady.
5. Drink of Lourdes water.
6. Pray Paradisus Dei's prayer for the New Springtime.
7. Do whatever God tells you.

TMIY

- How frequently do you say the Rosary? Are you willing to say it every day? Will you work to earn the "golden rosary?"

- Do you wear the Miraculous Medal? Are you willing to do so?

- How frequently do you go to Mass? Will you go more frequently?

- Will you join Amici di Giuseppe?

- Will you become a Missionary to the Family?

Next Week

The New Springtime

The New Springtime of the Church

The Mystery of Paradise

The Garden of Eden	Agony in the Garden	Resurrection in the Garden	The Eschatological Garden
"The LORD God planted a garden in Eden, in the east" (Genesis 2:8).	"There was a garden, which he and his disciples entered" (John 18:1).	"In the place where he was crucified there was a garden" (John 19:41).	"Then he showed me... the tree of life" (Revelation 22:1-2).

The Temple

The Church

The Holy Family

A Period of Peace

"The Old Testament comprises two times: before the Law, and under the Law. In the New Testament, likewise, there are two corresponding times: the time of the calling of the Gentiles that corresponds to the first, and the time of the calling of the Jews that corresponds to the second. This time is not yet, for then will be fulfilled these words of Isaiah: 'One nation shall not raise the sword against another, nor shall they train for war again' (Isaiah 2:4). For this is not yet fulfilled since... there are still disputes and heresies. Hence the Jews, who are waiting for this [the coming of the time of peace] believe Christ has not yet come" (15:24).

"In the end, my Immaculate Heart will triumph. The Holy Father will consecrate Russia to me, and she will be converted, and a period of peace will be granted to the world" (Our Lady, Fatima, July 13, 1917).

Source: Bonaventure, Collationes in Hexaemeron, The Works of Bonaventure, v. 5, St. Anthony Guild Press.
Fatima in Lucia's own Words," edited by Fr. Louis Kondor, SVD, The Ravengate Press, 1989, p. 105

The Four Leadership Roles of Men

Political Leadership	Harmoniously order society to peace.	**Moral Leadership** — Live in union with God to receive His blessings.
Economic Leadership	Make the earth fruitful, which is tied to the fruitfulness of the womb.	**Military Leadership** — Battle Satan over the family, the channel of grace.

Men's Leadership Roles

TMIY

Apostles of a New Springtime for the Church

"They will be true apostles of the latter times... They will have the two-edged sword of the Word of God in their mouths and the blood–stained standards of the Cross on their shoulders. They will carry the crucifix in their right hand and the rosary in their left, and the holy names of Jesus and Mary on their heart... Such are the great men who are to come" (St. Louis de Montfort, True Devotion to Mary).

"This order is understood through John to whom it was said, 'I wish him to remain until I come'" (St. Bonaventure, Collation 20.29).

"Peter turned and saw following them the disciple whom Jesus loved... When Peter saw him, he said to Jesus, 'Lord, what about this man?' Jesus said to him, 'If it is my will that he remain until I come, what is that to you? Follow me.' The saying spread abroad among the brethren that this disciple was not to die" (John 21:20-23).

Source: St. Louis de Montfort, "True Devotion to Mary," from "God Alone – The Collected Writings of St. Louis Marie de Montfort," Montfort Publications, Bayshore, NY, 1987, pp. 306-307.
Bonaventure, Collationes in Hexaemeron, The Works of Bonaventure, v. 5, St. Anthony Guild Press, Paterson, N.J., 1970, Collation 13.7, p. 186 and Collation 23.4, p. 316.

TMIY

The Gifts to Peter and John

"You are Peter, and on this rock I will build my church, and the powers of death shall not prevail against it" (Matthew 16:18).

"Simon, son of John, do you love me more than these?... Feed my lambs" (John 21:15).

"When Jesus saw his mother, and the disciple whom he loved standing near, he said to his mother, "Woman, behold, your son!" Then he said to the disciple, "Behold, your mother!" And from that hour the disciple took her to his own home" (John 19:26-27).

"[Joseph] did as the angel of the Lord commanded him; he took his wife" (Matthew 1:24).

TMIY

The Last Supper

"The disciples looked at one another, uncertain of whom he spoke. One of his disciples, whom Jesus loved, was lying close to the breast of Jesus; so Simon Peter beckoned to him and said, "Tell us who it is of whom he speaks." So lying thus, close to the breast of Jesus, he said to him, "Lord, who is it?"" (John 13:22-25).

John is part of the company of apostles united and obedient to its head: Peter.

The domestic Church is part of the universal Church and is obedient to the Pope.

The domestic Church has a special intimacy with Christ.

TMIY

The Foot of the Cross

"Truly, truly, I say to you, the cock will not crow, till you have denied me three times" (*John 13:38*).

"When Jesus saw his mother, and the disciple whom he loved standing near, he said to his mother, "Woman, behold, your son!" Then he said to the disciple, "Behold, your mother!" And from that hour the disciple took her to his own home" (*John 19:26-27*).

"The family is placed at the heart of the great struggle between good and evil, between life and death, between love and all that is opposed to love" (Pope John Paul II, *Letter to Families, #23*).

TMIY

Easter Morning: The Race to the Tomb

"Peter then came out with the other disciple, and they went toward the tomb. They both ran, but the other disciple outran Peter and reached the tomb first; and stooping to look in, he saw the linen cloths lying there, but he did not go in. Then Simon Peter came, following him, and went into the tomb" (*John 20:3-6*).

"The future of the world and of the Church pass by way of the family" (Pope John Paul II, *Familiaris Consortio, #75*).

The Church is the guardian of the mystery of salvation.

TMIY

The Life of St. Peter

- Makes missionary journeys from Jerusalem.
- Establishes the Church in Antioch with primacy among the Orthodox Churches.
- Establishes Church in Rome, which is the seat of the Western Church.
- Writes the 1st and 2nd Letters of Peter while in Rome.
- Martyred on the Vatican Hill outside Rome in the year 67AD.
- Rome becomes the seat of the hierarchical Church – residence of Pope.
- Churches are primarily named after the apostles/great saints of Christian history.
- The Seven Major Basilicas: St. John Lateran; St. Peter's Basilica; St. Paul outside the Walls; St. Mary Major; St. Lawrence outside the Walls; The Basilica of the Holy Cross in Jerusalem; St. Sebastian at the Catacombs.
- Holy Family is amazingly hidden. No Church for St. Joseph. He's hidden among the statues on colonnade. Originally, no statue of Our Lady. JPII added mosaic.

The Life of St. John

- Becomes Bishop of Church at Ephesus. Empty tomb is at Ephesus.
- House of St. John and Our Lady at Ephesus discovered by Abbe Julien Gouyet in 1881.
- Our Lady is proclaimed the "Theotokos" by the Council of Ephesus in 431 AD.
- Writes – 4th Gospel, 3 letters and the Book of Revelation.
- St. John consecrates St. Polycarp as the Bishop of Smyrna.
- St. Polycarp sends St. Pothinus to become the Bishop of Lyon, France. St. Pothinus is martyred in 177 AD.
- St. Pothinus is succeeded by St. Irenaeus, another disciple of St. Polycarp.
- St. Denis sent by Pope Fabian to become 1st Bishop of Paris, martyred ~ 250 AD.
- Clovis, the 1st king of a united France, is baptized in 496 AD by St. Remigius.
- France becomes the "eldest daughter of the Church."

The Church in France

- Gothic architecture is born at St. Denis in Paris: 80 Cathedrals and 500 large churches are built between 1050 – 1350.
- Reaches culmination in Notre Dame de Chartres, built to house the Sancta Camisa.
- "To us, it is a child's fancy; a toy-house to please the Queen of Heaven, to please her so much that she would be happy in it, to charm her till she smiled... If you are to get the full enjoyment of Chartres, you must... believe in Mary as Bernard... and feel her presence as the architects did, in every stone they placed, and every touch they chiseled" (Henry Adams).
- The Papacy moves to Avignon from 1309-1376.
- Three ecumenical councils are hosted in France: First Lyon (1245), Second Lyon (1274), and Vienne (1311-1312).
- The French played a crucial role in the launching of the First and Second Crusades.
- Three ecumenical councils are hosted in France: First Lyon (1245), Second Lyon (1274), and Vienne (1311-1312).

Source: Adams, H., "Mont Saint Michel and Chartres," Penguin Classics, 1986, pp. 88-96.

A Role for the United States

- The "New World" was discovered on Oct. 12, 1492 by Christopher Columbus sailing on the Santa Maria.

- First contact with the mainland was made on June 24, 1497 (Feast of St. John the Baptist) by John Cabot, a member of the Confraternity of St. John the Evangelist.

- The bishops of the United States unanimously selected Our Lady, under the title of The Immaculate Conception, as the Patroness of America on May 13, 1846.

- The choice was approved by Blessed Pope Pius IX on February 7, 1847.

- The consecration was most recently renewed on November 11, 2006.

- After Texas War of Independence, Texas was designated an Apostolic Prefecture in 1839.

- Fr. Jean Marie Odin arrives from Lyon, France in 1840.

- Fr. Odin is consecrated Bishop of the Vicariate Apostolic in 1842.

- Fr. Odin becomes the 1st Bishop of the Diocese of Galveston in 1847.

- St. Mary's Church in Galveston is established as the Cathedral and the Diocese is consecrated to Our Lady, under the title of The Immaculate Conception.

TMIY

SESSION 25

THAT MAN IS YOU!

- Have you ever heard about the special spiritual role that the United States has? What is your personal part in this special role?

- Could you answer the call like Paul?

- What is the most important thing you heard during this novena?

- What is the most important thing you've promised to do?

Next Week

That Man is You!
Taking the Next Step

That Man is You!
Taking the Next Step

The Path of Mercy for King David

1 King David Needed Mercy — "Nathan said to David, 'That man is you!'" (2 Samuel 12:7).

2 King David Encountered God — Have mercy on me, O God according to thy steadfast love; according to thy abundant mercy blot out my transgressions" (Psalm 51:1).

3 King David was Transformed — I have found in David the son of Jesse a man after my heart, who will do all my will" (Acts 13:22).

TMIY

The Four Leadership Roles of Men

Political Leadership — Harmoniously order society to peace.

Moral Leadership — Live in union with God to receive His blessings.

Men's Leadership Roles

Economic Leadership — Make the earth fruitful, which is tied to the fruitfulness of the womb.

Military Leadership — Battle Satan over the family, the channel of grace.

TMIY

The Path of That Man is You!

Year 1	Becoming a Man After God's Own Heart	Our relationship with God
Year 2	The Battle Over the Bride	Our relationship with our spouse
Year 3	The Revelation of the Father	Our relationship with our children

TMIY

The Mystery of St. Joseph

1	Relationship to God the Father	"Joseph, being a just man... resolved to send Mary away quietly" (Matthew 1:19).
2	Relationship to His Spouse	"The angel Gabriel was sent from God to a city of Galilee named Nazareth, to a virgin betrothed to a man whose name was Joseph" (Luke 1:26-27).
3	Relationship to His Adopted Son	"And when they saw him they were astonished; and his mother said to him, 'Son, why have you treated us so? Behold, your father and I have been looking for you anxiously'... and Jesus... was obedient to them" (Luke 2:48-51).

TMIY

Holy Family   Seven Steps

Holy Family		Seven Steps
The Niddah Laws (Cf. Leviticus 15:19)	1	Honor your wedding vows
Separation of the Challah (Cf. Numbers 15:20)	2	Use money for others
The Nerot Laws (Exodus 20:8)	3	Give God some of your time
The angel is sent to open Mary and Joseph's mind to God's presence in the home	4	Set your mind on things above
Mary is told she will find God in herself	5	Find God in yourself
Joseph is told he will find God in another person	6	Find God in other people
The Christian home is born when Joseph chooses the pathway to mercy and receives Mary into his home	7	Practice Superabundant Mercy

TMIY

Forming a Family

7 Steps: "Divorce Proofing" Marriage

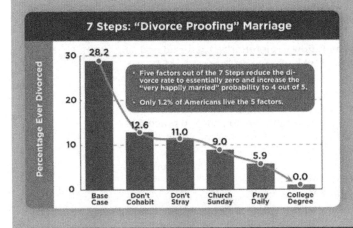

- Five factors out of the 7 Steps reduce the divorce rate to essentially zero and increase the "very happily married" probability to 4 out of 5.
- Only 1.2% of Americans live the 5 factors.

Percentage Ever Divorced:
- Base Case: 28.2
- Don't Cohabit: 12.6
- Don't Stray: 11.0
- Church Sunday: 9.0
- Pray Daily: 5.9
- College Degree: 0.0

Millennials and the 5 Factors

- Never married millennials live the 5 Factors at significantly lower levels.
- Do not cohabitate: Approximately 20%
- Pornography(weekly): M-41%; W-19%.
- Attend church weekly: M-13.6%;
- Pray daily: M-38.5%; W-43.0%.
- College degree: M-27.2%; W-35.0%

Source: Paradisus Dei. General Social Survey, 1972-2016.

TMIY

The Mystery of Paradise

The Garden of Eden	Agony in the Garden	Resurrection in the Garden	The Eschatological Garden
"The LORD God planted a garden in Eden, in the east" (Genesis 2:8).	"There was a garden, which he and his disciples entered" (John 18:1).	"In the place where he was crucified there was a garden" (John 19:41).	"Then he showed me... the tree of life" (Revelation 22:1-2).

The Temple

The Church

The Holy Family

TMIY

The Climactic Confrontation

"In our times evil has grown disproportionately, operating through perverted systems which have practiced violence and elimination on a vast scale... The evil of the twentieth century was not a small-scale evil, it was not simply 'homemade.' It was an evil of gigantic proportions."

"The aspiration that humanity nurtures... is the hope of a new civilization marked by freedom and peace. But for such an undertaking, a new generation of builders is needed... You are the men and women of tomorrow. The future is in your hearts and in your hands. God is entrusting to you the task... of working with him in the building of the civilization of love."

Sources: World Youth Day, Toronto, 2002. Pope St. John Paul II, "Memory and Identity," Rizzoli, New York, 2005, p. 167.

TMIY

Guiding the Family in Stormy Waters

"The Eucharist is the very source of Christian marriage... In this sacrifice of the New and Eternal Covenant, Christian spouses encounter the source from which their own marriage covenant flows, is interiorly structured and continuously renewed" (Pope St. John Paul II, *Familiaris Consortio, #57*).

"A number of historical circumstances also make a revival of the Rosary quite timely... The family, the primary cell of society, [is] increasingly menanced by forces of distintegration on both the ideological and practical planes, so as to make us fear for the future of this fundamental and indispensible institution and, with it, for the future of society as a whole. The revival of the Rosary in Chrsitian families... will be an effective aid to countering the devastating effects of this crisis typical of our age" (Pope St. John Paul II, *Rosarium Virginis Mariae, #6*).

TMIY

The Importance of the Holy Family

 It is in the Holy Family, the original 'Church in miniature (*Ecclesia Domestica*)', that every Christian family must be reflected. Through God's mysterious design, it was in that family that the Son of God spent long years of a hidden life. It is therefore the prototype and example for all Christian families.

St. John Paul II
Redemptoris Custos, #7

TMIY

Amici di Giuseppe – Friends of Joseph

1 Live the 7 Steps of Paradisus Dei/TMIY according to the heart of St. Joseph.
- "I have called you friends" (John 15:15).
- Entry into a deeper, contemplative spirituality based on the model of St. Joseph where science gives way to the science of love.
- Daily Rosary: "To contemplate the face of Christ and contemplate it with Mary."
- Monthly/weekly messages at the "school of Mary and Joseph."

2 Gather together with other Amici di Giuseppe men at least once/month for prayer and discussion.
- "Small combat group" meets at least monthly.
- Prayer: Mass and/or Rosary.
- Discussion/support in living the 7 Steps.

3 Enroll through the TMIY app or online.
- Possibility of connecting with other Amici di Giuseppe members.

4 Sign of membership.
- A specifically designed Amici di Giuseppe Rosary.

TMIY

Missionaries to the Family

1 The program will be a rigorous 1 year formation program.

2 University level intellectual formation will be online.

3 The Paradisus Dei spiritual formation will be both online and include weekend retreats.

4 Space is limited.

5 Application is required.

6 Ability to nominate other men.

7 If you or someone you know might be interested, please contact us.

TMIY

 TMIY
THAT MAN IS YOU!

SESSION 26

• How can you join together with other men to continue the journey? Will you join Amici di Giuseppe? Is God calling you to be a missionary?

• What is the most important insight through the That Man is You! program? How has That Man is You! changed your life?

Next Year

The Vision of Man Fully Alive

NOTES

NOTES

NOTES

NOTES

NOTES

Suggested Additional Reading

Secular

1. The Case for Marriage – Linda Waite and Christine Gallagher
2. The Index of Leading Cultural Indicators – William J. Bennett
3. Children, Adolescents and the Media – Victor C. Strasburger
4. Good to Great – Jim Collins
5. A Treatise on the Family – Gary S. Becker
6. The Rise of Christianity – Rodney Stark
7. Fewer: How the new Demography of Depopulation will Shape our Future – Ben J. Wattenburg
8. Father Facts – National Fatherhood Initiative – Wade F. Horn and Tom Sylvester
9. Soft Porn Plays Hardball – Judith A. Reismann
10. The Medical Consequences of Loneliness – James J. Lynch
11. The High Price of Materialism – Tim Kasser

Religious

1. Mother Teresa: Come Be My Light – Brian Kolodiejchuck
2. Memory and Identity – Pope John Paul II
3. Joseph of Nazareth – Federico Suarez
4. Fatima, Russia and the Pope – Timothy Tindal-Robertson
5. Confessions – St. Augustine
6. Crossing the Threshold of Hope – Pope John Paul II
7. The Voyage to Lourdes – Alexis Carrel/Stanley L. Jaki
8. The Story of a Soul – St. Therese of Lisieux
9. Lectio Divina and the Practice of Teresian Prayer – Institute of Carmelite Studies
10. Give Me Souls: The Life of Don Bosco – Father Peter Lappin
11. Wherever He Goes – Fr. Marie Dominique Philippe
12. The Practice of the Presence of God – Brother Lawrence of the Resurrection
13. Divine Mercy in My Soul – St. Faustina Kowalska

Church Documents

1. The Catechism of the Catholic Church
2. Compendium of the Social Doctrine of the Church
3. Dives in Misericordia – Pope John Paul II
4. Novo Millennio Ineunte, Pope John Paul II
5. Redemptoris Hominis - Pope John Paul II
6. Gratissimam Sane – Pope John Paul II

Made in the USA
Columbia, SC
10 August 2019